Foreword

This is a short account of how two large suburbs grew up from small villages in less than a hundred years, written principally for past and present Broughton and Cheetham residents and others who work, shop or visit friends here. It all happened in the nineteenth century and, although many dynamic changes have taken place in our own times, the pattern of these districts was complete a long time ago. I wish to acknowledge the ready assistance I have received in the course of my researches from the staffs of the Local History Libraries, in particular from Mr John Shirt and Mr Tony Frankland of Salford, Mr David Taylor of Manchester and Mr Wilkinson at Prestwich. I have also received encouragement from the well-known Local Historians Mr Chris Makepeace and Mr Bill Williams.

Although no book has hitherto been written on the history of either Broughton or Cheetham Hill, I have made use of references by the following:

T Swindells: Manchester Streets and Manchester Men
Louis M Hayes: Reminiscences of Manchester
L H Grindon: Manchester Banks and Bankers
G Middleton: Annals òf Prestwich
S W Partington: Toll Bars of Manchester
James Ogden: Manchester 100 Years Ago

Periodicals:
The Sphinx, The Jackdaw, Manchester Faces and Places, Manchester City News, City Lantern

My wife's interest and encouragement has been a major factor in my work and I dedicate this, my first literary effort, to her.

Monty Dobkin

Country Villages

In 1801, when the first national census was taken, Manchester's population was 70,409. At that time both Cheetham and Broughton were separate townships, with only 752 and 866 residents respectively, although Manchester was no bigger in area than either of them. Prestwich, a parish in its own right with an ancient church and a long recorded history, boasted 1,811 inhabitants. Salford, like Manchester, had a large population crowded into a small area.

The outer districts, beginning at Strangeways, were open countryside comprising fields, farms and meadow and even the River Irwell was a pleasant stream. Much of the land was owned by a few wealthy families whose ancestors had claimed it centuries earlier, such as the Egertons of Heaton Park (later Earls of Wilton), Lord Ducie of Strangeways Hall, the Chethams of Crumpsall Hall and Smedley Hall, the Clowes of Broughton Old Hall and the Byroms of Kersal Cell. At the beginning of the nineteenth century only one road led to town, the Bury Old Road, which was turnpiked in 1754 and passed through Heaton Park, Cheetham Hill and Red Bank. There was little wheeled traffic; people did not go far from their homes and the few cross country lanes sufficed for the needs of the local residents. To reach Broughton they used Halliwell Lane, Tetlow Lane and Broom Lane and to reach Prestwich, Ostrich Lane and Rectory Lane. Their occupations were mostly smallholdings and cottage industries associated with textile production. Looking after a cow, a few pigs or hens and some hand spinning or weaving were the daily tasks of the common people. Their lives had changed little in centuries and until the middle of the eighteenth century they felt certain that no changes were ever likely to occur. Although within so short a distance, by our standards, of the sizeable towns of Manchester and Salford, they had little occasion to visit these places from which they were worlds apart. The

great event of the ye[...] which meant that larg[...] miles around turned [...] gigantic fairground for [...] the middle 1680's, the [...] and usually took pl[...] authorities consider th[...] the forerunner of Manch[...]

In an account of an outing to the races, written by an octogenarian late in the nineteenth century, the author recalled walking with his mates from Manchester through Strangeways en route for Kersal Moor early in the century:

"An extensive meadow almost reaching from Cheetwood Lane as far as the present (c1890) Waterloo Road was covered with rich grass, the hawthorn's rich scent perfuming the air. The road is in a tolerable condition as far as the corner of Broughton Lane. After this we are soon in Stony Knolls, a mere good road, a beaten track over hill and valley until we reach Cliff Point, the junction of Lower Broughton Road with the road to Cheetham Hill and Prestwich. Here we enter a sandy lane and in the side nearest the river are a few old houses, one of them a public house nicknamed 'Hard Backed Nan's'. In the valley nestles a comfortable farmstead...We pursue our way through this sandy lane and on a narrow road without even a footpath.

A little higher up on this road the vehicles from Manchester are entering the crowded road from Singleton Brook, the highway for carriages to the race course from the town being by way of Millers Lane, Long Millgate, Scotland Bridge and hence through Cheetham Hill..."

Sporting activities were very limited, but in one popular sphere Broughton, Cheetham Hill and Prestwich too were renowned for their sportsmen. This was the pastime of archery which, having been a martial art for centuries in the Middle Ages, continued as a village sport long after its practice in wartime had been superseded. Even after it was in decline in other areas it maintained its popularity here. A great local archer, James Rawson (1715-1795), was well known as a countrywide unbeaten champion. The Robin Hood Inn, opposite Crescent Road, was a local meeting place for archers, as was Butt Hill in Prestwich.

In his poem, "Archery", written in 1793, James Ogden, a Manchester writer and poet, speaks of:

The Broughton Archers, and the Bowmen good
Of Lancashire, keep up their former name
Their sires acquir'd, for skill in archery;
Ennobled Egerton, of Heaton-House,
These Patronizes, bearing for his crest,
Three pheon'd arrows with a ribbon bound...

...Near Manchester at Chetham Butts they meet,
Chetham, long famous for an archer race,
The Rawsons, brethren dext'rous in the art,
John, Roger, Daniel, known at meetings round,
For upwards of an hundred years by past,
By all acknowledg'd masters of the bow;
And James, the son of John, when in his prime,
Refus'd no challenge, nor a match e'er lost...

...Near Kersal Moor the Broughton Archers fix
their targets, pierced with many a well-aimed shot

During this period, archery had been revived by the Prince of Wales (subsequently George IV), and nowhere in England did the old flame burst out more brightly than in our own neighbourhood. "On Wednesday last," says Harrop on October 16th 1792, "the Lancashire Bowmen met at Cheetham Hill to shoot for their annual prize, an elegant bugle-horn, presented by John Dixon, Esq." The club, called the "Broughton Archers", was instituted in the early days of the nineteenth century, perhaps even earlier, and was composed exclusively of gentlemen - Church-and-King men (Conservatives, as they would now be termed) of the old school.

In the 1830's they were men who represented the weight and influence of the town. Among them were Mr J C Harter, Canon Parkinson, Mr Richard Barton, Mr John Barton, Mr Hardman, Mr Gilbert Winter, Mr Joseph Winter, Mr J Bradshaw Wanklyn, Captain Hindley, Mr Entwistle, Mr James Crossley, Mr T S Scholes, Dr R F Ainsworth, Mr Edward Loyd secundus and Messrs Oliver and Arthur Heywood, who reckoned as juniors.

Originally, the rendezvous was in the archery ground adjoining "Nan's", the celebrated old country tavern, just above Broken Brow, the site of which became the residence of the Bishop of Manchester. Before the construction of Bury New Road, "Nan's" was comparatively secluded, and when it became too public, the club shifted to the Turf Tavern, Kersal Moor, which belonged at that time to the Rev John Clowes. He added a large dining room to the tavern for the use of the club, of which he was a member. The chimney piece, under Mr Clowes' directions, was ornamented with a frieze representing archery practice, and at the upper end of the room was a portrait of Sir Ashton Lever, once the ruling spirit of local archery. He was represented as engaging in "clout shooting", which was one of the favourite old methods of acquiring skill. A sheet was suspended some distance from the archer, so that the flight of the arrow had to be a parabola, which required precise calculation.

In the early years of the eighteenth century, life in country villages and the small market towns continued as it had done for generations past, but by the middle of the century many changes were on the way. Before the century ended the world was a very different place and even the remote villages knew that things would never be the same again.

The Industrial Revolution – new inventions enabling people to produce goods in new ways – was a very English revolution. It was not bred of violence or oppression or poverty; the English character seized the opportunities created by inventive genius and led the world in manufacturing more products, in larger quantities and much more quickly than had ever been thought possible. The results were good for some – not so good for many others.

The first beneficiaries of the great changes in South Lancashire were the merchants, the men who organised production and sold it at home and abroad. They supplied the raw materials to cottage workers in their various trades of spinning, weaving and other processes, collected the pieces for finishing and brought them to their warehouses in Manchester. They had agents in many parts of the world and by their enterprise grew very rich. Factories were built, usually near streams to provide power, and soon villagers were forced to work in these factories instead of in their own homes. Manchester soon became very populous: people left the villages, seeking work, and then Irish immigrants flooded in as cheap labour. But Broughton, Cheetham Hill and Prestwich were very little affected by this aspect of the Industrial Revolution, as these areas had been chosen by the Manchester merchants for their country homes. They joined the landed gentry by purchasing large estates and building spacious mansions in private parks, yet they were within driving distance of their warehouses and factories. As these areas lacked many of the facilities which had attracted the first factories, they were kept free of industry and of other great changes, so preserving the way of life which the merchants and landowners wanted for their own enjoyment. Thus the early character of these districts as residential suburbs was established.

The 70,000 people in Manchester were crowded into a very small area of today's inner city; along the banks of the Irwell from Victoria Station to Bridge Street and as far as Ancoats, Shudehill and Albert Square. The squalid living and working conditions have been described by many writers. A very short distance away the picture was vastly different. Interspersed in great open spaces were a number of long established settlements, the oldest of which was close to Prestwich Parish Church. There were groups of cottages in Rooden near today's Whittaker Lane, Rainsough, the Cliff, Cheetham Hill, Smedley Lane and Cheetwood and these were the main populated areas, while the stately homes in their many acres of gardens and grounds occupied most of the rest of the landscape. The population had been so sparse that, until 1790, when St Mark's Church was built at a cost of £2,000, a writer in "Manchester Faces and Places" could say:

Halliwell Lane, where c1788 James Halliwell built one of the first mansions in Cheetham Hill, Broomfield

"Such was the spiritual destitution of the benighted folk of Cheetham Hill, Crumpsall and Broughton that between the ancient parish churches of Prestwich and Manchester there was neither a place for divine worship nor for interment of the dead."

Being situated close to the boundary where Cheetham and Broughton meet, St Mark's served both townships for the next half century until St John's, Broughton, and St Luke's, Cheetham, were built.

Cheetwood – An Urban Village

Cheetwood is now only a name and a faint memory to older people, but it was once a well populated village between Strangeways and what became Hightown. It was a very pretty village too, with quaint cottages and well tended gardens. About 1900 Swindells, in "Manchester Streets and Manchester Men", gave us a delightful description:

"The title urban village is apparently a contradictory one, but I think I can show that as applied to Cheetwood it is quite correct. To the visitor of today the place has not the charm that it had for our grandfathers, but it remains yet a little community standing by itself...From the heights of Cheetwood you can look down upon the surrounding town, and from no part of the village can the view be described as picturesque. Brick crofts monopolise the view on the one side, whilst in the direction of the Bury New Road the outlook is over rows of uninteresting houses, whose blue slate roofs and smoking chimneys are a poor substitute for the expanse of gardens and fields that met the eye sixty years ago.

In those days, although brick making had made its appearance in the vicinity, Cheetwood was a pleasant place to live in. The tea gardens, which were about midway through the village, was a popular place of resort in summer times. Loving couples would on Sundays and other holidays find their way thither, there to enjoy to a modified degree the pleasures of country life. Tea could be partaken of in the little summer houses that were dotted up and down the gardens, which were gay with numberless flowers; and the air was sweet with the perfume of roses, pinks, carnations, mignonette, and other blooms. At midsummer the smell of new mown hay was wafted from the adjoining fields, and in the breeze met the eye. In the orchards the currant and gooseberry trees bore many a fine crop of fruit; and when the summer was on the wane the overhanging branches of pear and apple trees offered abundant temptation to the juveniles of the hamlet. Tea taken amidst such surroundings was a delight to hundreds of town dwellers, who would often carry home with them to their cottages in overcrowded streets, souvenirs of their holiday in the shape of bunches of fragrant blooms. The village consisted of one street, which terminated in Dirty Lane, under which designation present-day residents will fail to recognise Elizabeth Street. Dirty Lane did not belie its name. It lived up to its reputation and was known, for one period at any rate, for the deepness of its cart ruts, which in the winter time caused the lane to be a veritable slough of despond. It was originally nothing more than an occupation road giving access to the fields that bounded it, and the farms to which they belonged.

Leaving Dirty Lane, Wilton Terrace would be passed. Built in 1836, the houses for many years overlooked open fields which extended to Collyhurst. Behind the terrace more open fields, with the pleasant village of Cheetwood on the one hand and the wooded heights of Higher Broughton on the other, made residence there more than tolerable. Beyond Wilton Terrace there were very few houses, the land on either side being devoted to agriculture. The Temple and the bowling green connected therewith, together with St Luke's Church, were notable landmarks.

In Smedley there were large houses commanding magnificent views towards the hills and a clear view of smoky Manchester a little over a mile away. From the corner where Smedley Lane now meets Cheetham Hill Road until a little way before Crescent Road, there were only half a dozen residences but each was situated in extensive acreage. The best known was Greenhill, which name is well preserved to this day. This was the home of Samuel Jones, one of the earliest bankers whose partner was his kinsman Edward Loyd. Their premises in King Street is still a bank to this day – the Loyd Entwistle branch of the National Westminster Bank; the name of Samuel Jones's original bank is commemorated there in view of all passers-by.

One of Manchester's greatest benefactors, Thomas Henshaw, was an early resident of Cheetham Hill, his mansion, Stonewall, adjoining Greenhill opposite Halliwell Lane. He was in business in Oldham as a felt hat manufacturer. When he died in 1810 he left £20,000 to found an institution for the blind and the name Henshaw has ever since been synonymous with assistance in this direction. He left a similar sum to found a Blue Coat School for boys in Oldham.

Halliwell Lane owes its name to James Halliwell, who purchased land in 1788 behind the Griffin Hotel and built Broomfield, which was approached by a farm track. Other prosperous merchants also built houses here; Oakhill was erected soon after Broomfield, as were three or four mansions a little further along in Tetlow Fold. The farm track was widened to allow the carriages access to these estates and these became the homes of the most prominent magnates of the times.

The Old Families

Heaton Park was the ancestral home of the Egerton family, who had acquired it by marriage in 1684. A hall had stood on the site for many years and in 1772 Sir Thomas Egerton MP built the present Heaton Hall, which remained the home of the Earls of Wilton, as they became, until 1902. In that year Manchester Corporation bought the 600 acres together with the Hall for £230,000. The Egertons were an aristocratic family with a long pedigree and were related by marriage to many other noble families. Much has been written about their lives and activities and, as the most important people for miles around, they played leading roles in the life of the community for generations.

Broughton Park occupied the entire area from Singleton Road to Broom Lane, with Broughton Old Hall, the residence of the Lord of the Manor, at its centre. Broughton with Kersal had descended from the Stanleys to the Chethams, but when Edward Chetham died in 1772 his sister, Mary Clowes, succeeded to the Hall, the Lordship of the Manor and the ownership of over 1,000 acres. Until 1801, when his son Samuel died and was succeeded by his grandson, also Samuel Clowes, there was no other building in the whole area of the park. About this time they built a new hall but, for some reason not recorded, the Clowes family never occupied the New Hall and it was let to well chosen tenants ever afterwards. For the next half century no other building was erected in the park limits.

Adjoining both Heaton Park at one end and Broughton Park at the other was the Sedgley Tenement, afterwards known as Sedgley Park. From

Scholes Lane to the Singleton Brook, the boundary of Prestwich and Broughton, the 97 acres with Sedgley House were bought in 1777 by Thomas Philips, one of the early prosperous Manchester merchants whose family firm, J & N Philips, flourished until recent times. The entrance drive to the Hall was on Bury Old Road near Kings Road.

High Bank, at the junction of Bury Old Road and Scholes Lane, was built in the mid eighteenth century as the residence of Thomas Scholes, a member of a very old Prestwich family whose name is commemorated in the Lane where their principal residences stood. We are fortunate that High Bank has been preserved as Nazareth House and is a beautiful example of Georgian architecture. Another family residence was Woodhill, demolished in the 1920's and replaced by Woodhill Drive and surrounding avenues of modern villas.

Stocks House stood for nearly 300 years where North Street joins Cheetham Hill Road and was very isolated. There were a few small houses at the bottom of Red Bank and some large residences in Smedley Lane, but Stocks House was alone in its many acres of grounds. The estate appears to have extended about 130 yards east of the high road and to have been about the same length north to south. There were several outbuildings and the grounds were laid out in an ornamental manner with gardens, shrubberies, ponds and walks. One lake was serpentine in shape and was one hundred yards long. At the turn of the eighteenth century Stocks was a fine, roomy mansion, one portion of which was three storeys high and another two storeys. The family who owned the estate for many years was named Ryding, but little is known of their history and it is the nineteenth century owners of whom more is known and to whom reference will be made in later chapters.

Crumpsall Hall, the seat of the Chetham family, was situated in what is now Crescent Road and

Crumpsall Hall (demolished 1825) was the birth place of Humphrey Chetham. It was situated just off Crescent Road

stood there for some three hundred years before it was pulled down in 1825. Humphrey Chetham, perhaps the most famous member of this illustrious family, died in 1653 leaving a fortune for charitable purposes; his trustees were able to endow the school which still flourishes in the centre of Manchester. Originally a Blue Coat School for orphans, its purpose was changed in recent times and it is now one of the principal schools of music in the United Kingdom. Another seat of the Chethams was Smedley Old Hall and their land-holdings were spread over many districts.

The history of Kersal Cell has been told so often that it is the best known of the old buildings which have been preserved through the ages. It was the home of one of the leading familes, the

Broughton Old Hall, ancestral Home of the Clowes family. The lake is still a well-known feature of the Park

Pedigree of Clowes, of Broughton Hall.

Samuel Clowes, of Manchester, was, at the date of his will, = **Ann**, daughter of Roger 15 August, 1727 (proved 22 January, 1747), lord of the | Meakin, of Manchester, manor of Booths, co. Lancaster, and possessed considerable | gent. landed property in Manchester, Gorton, Worsley, and Til-desley, co. Lancaster.

Samuel Clowes, of Ridgefield, = **Mary**, sister and | **Thomas Clowes.** | **John Clowes**, of Ridgefield, Man- | 4. **Joseph Clowes.** | **Anne**, mar-afterwards of Chadwick, and | co-heiress of | | chester, married Eleanor, daughter | 5. **William Clowes.** | ried to Sam-finally of Smedley, co. Lan- | Edward Chet- | | of Richard Taylor, of the City of | | uel Birch, of caster, ob. July, 1773. | ham, Esq., of | | London, merchant, and left two | | Ardwick. | Castleton. | | daughters, his co-heiresses.

Samuel Clowes, Esq., of Broughton, = **Rachael**, daughter and co-heiress | **Edward** | **Mary**, married 1st to —— Hilton, Esq., co. Lancaster, High Sheriff, 1777, ob. | of William Legh, Esq., of West | died *s.p.* | and 2ndly to Thomas Cross, Esq., of 17 January, 1801. | Houghton. | | Shaw Hill, co. Lancaster (*see* that family).

Samuel Clowes, Esq., of Broughton, = **Martha**, daughter of | **William**, | **Mary**, married to John Livesey, Lieut.-Col. Royal Lancashire Fenci- | John Tipping, Esq., | died *s.p.* | Esq., of Blackburn. bles, married 10 February, 1774, ob. 5 | of Manchester, ob. | | **Frances**, married to Rev. Henry October, 1799. | 1790 | | Brown, of Firby.

Samuel Clowes, Esq., of Broughton, | Rev. **John Clowes**, of | **William Legh Clowes**, Esq., of Brough- = **Antonia Henrietta**, | **Mary**, married to General Sir co. Lancaster, and of Warmsworth | Broughton, M.A., and | ton, sometime Colonel in the army, born | daughter of Rev. | George Scovell, K.C.B., of Hall, co. York, born 1775, High | some time Fellow of | 9 March, 1781, who served with the 3rd | Charles Shuttleworth | Sandhurst, Berks. Sheriff, 1809; married, 1801, Dulci- | the Collegiate Church | Light Dragoons during the Peninsular | Holden, of Aston | **Martha**, married to her cousin bella, daughter of James Wilkinson, | in Manchester, born | War, and commanded that regiment at | Hall, co. Derby | Samuel Chetham Hilton, Esq. Esq., of Newcastle, and died *s.p.* 22 | 1777, died unmarried, | the battle of Salamanca, married 1818, ob. | | **Frances**, married to Rev. Joseph July, 1811. | 28 September, 1846. | 10 August, 1862. | | Bradshaw, M.A., rector of | | | | Wilmslow, co. Chester.

Samuel William Clowes = Hon. **Adelaide** | **John Clowes**, = **Caroline** | St. **John Legh Clowes**, of | **George Gooch Clowes**, | **Emma**, married to Rev. Atkinson An-Esq., of Broughton Hall, | **Cavendish**, | Esq., of Bur- | **Eliza-** | Cotgrave Place, co. Notts, | Major Worcester Yeo- | thony Holden, rector of Hawton, co. co. Lancaster, and of Wood- | 2nd daughter | ton Court, co. | **beth**, | born 1832, married 1856, | manry Cavalry, sometime | Notts. house Eaves, co. Leicester, | of Henry Man- | Hereford, | youngest | Hon. Elizabeth Caroline | Captain and Brevet-Major | **Henrietta Amelia**, married to Rev. Captain Leicestershire Yeo- | ners, 3rd Lord | J.P. and D.L. | daughter | Bingham, daughter of | 8th Hussars, born 1835, | J. C. Ryle, vicar of Stradbroke, co. manry • Cavalry, M.P. for | Waterpark, 2nd | born 25 Mar., | of P. Ark- | Denis Arthur, 3rd Lord | married, June, 1861, Susan | Suffolk. North Leicester, born 27 | wife, married | 1823, married | wright, | Clanmorris = | Caroline, eldest daughter | **Isabel**, married to J. C. Arkwright, Esq., January, 1821, married 1st, | 3 December, | 22 January, | Esq., of | | of Dr. J. C. Wigram, | and died 1855. (*See* pedigree of that 6 May, 1852, Sophia Louisa, | 1863. | 1852. | Willersley, | | Bishop of Rochester. | family.) 2nd daughter of the late Sir | | | co. Derby | | | **Rosamond Adelin**, married to Rev. F. Richard Sutton, Bart. (she | | | | | | C. Fisher, rector of Walton-on-Trent. died 18th February, 1853, | | | | **William Legh Clowes**, born 1860. | **Edith**, married to Hugh T. Hulton, Esq., having had an only son, who | | | | St. **John Henry Clowes**, born 1862. | 5th son of William Hulton, Esq., of died in infancy). | | | | **George Arthur Clowes**, born 1864. | Hulton Park. | | | | **Francis John Clowes**, born 1868. | | | | **Philip Cecil Clowes**, born January | | | | 30 1871, died same year. | | | | **Edith Maude**, born 1869. | | | | **Evelyn Mary**, born May 7, 1872.

Henry Arthur Clowes, | **Peter Legh Clowes**, born 30 August, 1853. | **Charles Edward Clowes**, born 28 July, 1858. born 7 May, 1867. | **John Fitzherbert Clowes**, born 29 July, 1856, | **Caroline Rachael.** | ob. 19 February, 1857. | **Susan Mary Marguerite.**

Byroms, in the seventeenth, eighteenth and nineteenth centuries and they exerted a considerable influence in all aspects of life in and around Manchester.

There is an air of old world charm along Lower Broughton Road from Great Cheetham Street to the Cliff and although it is wholly nineteenth century (with a little twentieth century added) the atmosphere is a reminder of much earlier times, when along the banks of the river there was a settled village life. In the seventeenth century Broughton Spout, as this spot was known, was the residence of a renowned astronomer, William Crabtree, who in 1639 observed and recorded the transit of Venus between the sun and the Earth,

a great scientific achievement which was acclaimed at home and abroad. Part of this area is often referred to as the Priory and although there is a public house of this name, there has never been a religious settlement here. The name derives from a large house built very early in the nineteenth century by James Harrop, a successful printer and owner of the Manchester Mercury, the principal local newspaper of the period 1752-1830. The house was known locally as Harrop's Folly, which seems to indicate that for some reason it excited more derision than admiration.

Another local landmark was also dubbed a folly – Yates's Folly. This was the black and white building, possibly dating from Tudor times, although not originally built on its present site. It is on record that in 1822, when Market Street was being widened, two houses were purchased by William Yates, a manufacturer of furnishing trimmings who lived in Newton Street. He had them re-erected in Broughton, well outside the town and in open country and lived there for several years. The house, known locally as Knolls House, was tenanted for several years afterwards.

The reputation of Strangeways has for so long been associated with the gloom and misery of the prison and the crowded slums of the turn of the century. It is difficult to believe that this area was once mostly occupied by a stately home and its beautiful park. From the sixteenth century Strangeways Hall and Park was the seat first of the Strangeways family and later of other landed families. In 1770 it was the home of Lord Ducie, whose descendants own a great deal of North Manchester and elsewhere to this day.

In the Manchester City News "Notes and Queries" in 1881, a correspondent, remembering the early years of the century, wrote of the Strangeways he

Kersal Cell

knew or heard of in his youth:

"From the heights of Strangeways Park, through deep and well-wooded cloughs ran streams of clear water to fill the ornamental ponds in the gardens of Strangeways Hall, a stately, partly modern, partly gable-ended mansion, with stately iron gates, now keeping watch and ward over the principal entrance to Peel Park. The Hall was the residence of Francis Reynolds, Esq, father of the first Lord Ducie. The present Lord Ducie is the owner of the Strangeways Estate.

At the Strangeways end of Broughton Lane were a few residences, and in the near fields there was a nest of working men's lock-up gardens, wherein many a rare pink and picotee and many a swelling stick of celery were nourished with fond and jealous care. The lane onwards was knee-deep in sand, and the resort of numerous small red and brown butterflies, which the lads called Red Drummers, till it joined the still lower road from Broughton Bridge, near the Suspension Bridge, and so by a few cottages to the Griffin Inn, the Cheetham Arms, and its opposite ford, a noted bathing-place for Manchester youths. Round about this locality were several farms and farmhouses, one especially (recently covered by Albert Park) lives in our remembrance as the pasture from which was taken each evening in summer time, more than a century ago, our ancestors' old mare, the first horse used in Manchester in a gin to turn a mill which perched or straightened the nap on the back of fustian pieces."

A Genteel Neighbourhood

The turnpike of the Cheetham Hill Trust which became Bury Old Road was the only direct route to Manchester for many years and its main features were the toll bars for the collection of fees and the public houses "for the refreshment of man and beast". At the junction of the Middleton Road stood the White Smithy Bar, a six-sided structure with a porch and side windows, constructed to enable the keeper to see in the directions of Bury, Middleton and Cheetham Hill. Nearby was the forge, which gave the place its name, and the Half Way House Inn appeared here many years later. There was also a toll bar, mostly for race week traffic at Singleton Road.

Temple toll bar was near Smedley Lane and its picture in Partington's "Toll Bars of Manchester" so greatly resembles the Temple Hotel as it is today that it is probable that when the toll was abolished the toll house became a public house. The Eagle and Child formerly stood on this spot and the bowling green is referred to in the writings of Samuel Bamford, the Lancashire poet. He was a witness of the Peterloo Massacre on 16th August 1819 and wrote that on his way home the next day he rested at the Eagle and Child and ate the sandwiches prepared for the previous day but, for obvious reasons, uneaten.

I have referred to the Robin Hood, which has stood on the same spot for 200 years as a rendezvous of sportsmen, but the social centre was the Griffin, nearer to Halliwell Lane. The present building is obviously a replacement of the original but it is on the same site. A charity ball which was held here in May 1820 is described in Wheeler's Manchester Chronicle, and it is probably typical of the time and the place:

"On Wednesday se'night the appointed Ball, in aid of the depressed fund for promoting the useful objects of St Mark's Sunday and Day Schools, was held at the Griffin Inn, and attended by no less than two hundred and eighty persons. This extensive party combined the rank and fashion of that genteel neighbourhood; of several adjacent towns; and of Manchester and Salford. The

Knolls House on Bury New Road was once known as Yates' Folly. It is now (1984) under threat of demolition

Stewards for managing this benevolent and pleasurable fete were the Rev J Clowes; Wm Jones, Chas Brandt and Wm Garnett, Esquires. A Committee was also appointed. These gentlemen received the active and kind assistance of the principal Ladies resident at Cheetham; and as the whole scheme of the undertaking was founded in charity and consequently in economy, the Stewards and the Committee felt that they owed much of their success to the exertions of their amiable supporters. The supper, the wines, the dessert, were to be gratuities; and the families of the vicinity supplied all these in the most abundant quantities, in order that the profits arising from the sale of tickets might be as much as possible untouched, and applied chiefly to the education of the rising generation. This was indeed a noble aim, worthy of those by whom the plan was originally suggested; and the Committee and the Stewards who undertook its fulfilment. Success crowned the scheme beyond anticipation; and whilst an evening was spent which yields to none of its kind for continued pleasure and complete enjoyment, the sum of one hundred guineas has been obtained for that most gratifying purpose, and in liquidation of a debt contracted in building the School.

The whole of the extensive Inn was called into request. Six rooms were occupied for dancing, cards, promenading, refreshments and supper. The company were most politely received by the Committee and by the Stewards. Many Clergymen and Military Officers attended; and the Ladies were dressed in the most brilliant style. The thronging groups formed a splendid assemblage of fashion and beauty; and the arrangements were worthy of the company. In the principal passage on the stair-case was placed a resplendent target of illuminated lamps. Lights, lustres and ingenious devices, met the eye in every direction in the avenues, forming a blaze of radiance. But when the parties were introduced into the Ball-room, a combination of taste and resplendence was encountered which baffles description. It was hung with elegant white drapery in waving festoons, ornamented by artificial flowers which vied with Nature, with real evergreens, and with ivyleaves. At each end of the room was a splendid mirror, encircled with fanciful wreaths of flowers; and the division of it for two dancing parties was managed by temporary columns, erected for the night, decorated with every device of taste and ingenuity, in flowers and evergreens. At one end an Orchestra was raised, occupied by an excellent band. And the whole was lighted with wax, in elegant chandeliers and branches, producing a high effect. This unexpected spectacle had been designed and executed by four young Ladies, to whom the Committee were indebted for the great labour bestowed upon it, and for its correct execution. In the Promenade-room was a handsome stand of beautiful plants, with which the Committee had been accommodated for the evening by a neighbouring Gentleman.

The country dances were commenced by Mr Wm Garnett and Miss Blackwall and were continued with great spirit till the announcement of the superb supper. The quadrille parties were kept up with no less animation in a room appropriated to them. The tables were arranged in three rooms on the ground floor, and were enriched with beautiful flowers, chiefly supplied from the gardens of Broughton and Smedley Halls. The skill with which this part of the entertainments was regulated, exceeds all praise. Abundance of viands, comprising an elegant cold collation, with choice wines, the whole furnished gratuitously by about thirty families, displayed in the most inviting manner, attracted the attention of the guests, of whom 140 sat down at one time with the most perfect order. The Ladies of the neighbourhood had done more than justice to this branch of the undertaking, which called forth a general expression of approbation from those who partook of it. Elegance, propriety and plenty went hand in hand in the arrangements. Afterward a second set of 140 sat down to the renewed bounties of the banquet. Dancing was again commenced, and continued with unabated energy till the morning dawn broke in upon the enjoyment. The company not till then retired, in every way recompensed for their attendance, and pronouncing the evening to have been one of the most agreeable and satisfactory they ever enjoyed; mirth and good humour having reigned in unallayed dominion throughout the whole of it.

On the following day the rooms were opened for the gratification of the working classes of Cheetham-Hill and the neighbourhood to whom also under the superintendence of the Ladies and Gentlemen who have conducted the whole, the surplus provision of the preceding night were liberally distributed. And on Sunday, that the diffusion of pleasure might be quite complete, each child educated in the School was complimented with a present of a bun. Thus, in the end, the rich and the poor were combined in our common feeling of satisfaction on the occasion."

This description tells us a great deal about the district and it is obvious that many people of rank and fortune were already well established residents. The Stewards were very prominent men in different spheres of life and wielded great

White Smithy Bar was at the junction of Bury Old Road and Middleton Road, now the site of the Half Way House

influence. Rev J Clowes was Lord of the Manor of Broughton, William Jones was a banker, Charles Brandt had been Boroughreeve and William Garnett was a very well known merchant and later a politician. Their sponsorship attracted a gathering of many of the top people for miles around – and the arrangements described proves that they really knew the right way to organise a high class ball! They also knew their duty to the poor and duly fed them with the leftovers.

This was 1820, by which date, despite the Napoleonic wars only a few years past, the cotton industry had boomed, steam power had taken over and bigger mills and factories were producing larger and larger quantities. Manchester's population was over 100,000 and increasing rapidly and, as it became more overcrowded, those who could afford houses outside the town began to move north and south. People were attracted to the open countryside of Chorlton on Medlock, Ardwick and Hulme as well as to Broughton, Cheetham and Prestwich. As the cotton trade thrived, other trades followed in its wake and many professions and skilled crafts were employed in developing the new techniques. The manufacture of machinery became in itself another major industry; surveyors, solicitors and architects were needed and to lubricate the wheels of industry, finance was essential. Banking developed greatly and in all spheres Manchester was a world centre. The heads of businesses and their families continued to build their own mansions but before long some of those a rung or two lower on the ladder were also enabled to live in the newly founded suburbs. Prosperous shopkeepers in Deansgate and Market Street felt that they no longer needed to live over the shop and they too moved out. The next twenty years saw more changes than the preceding 200 and by 1840 Manchester's population was over 200,000; that of Cheetham and Broughton together was about 10,000, an increase of 600% in forty years. It was a dramatic period in which the railways were born, Manchester and Salford elected their first MP's, Cheetham joined with Manchester to obtain Incorporation, omnibus services were started and two new roads were built.

Until 1820 all traffic going north from Manchester towards Middleton, Bury, Radcliffe and other mill towns passed through the very narrow Red Bank and North Street to join the turnpike near Elizabeth Street, but with the increase in trade a new and better road was needed. The River Irk had been crossed at Ducie Bridge (near Victoria Station) and a straight, wide road was completed in 1820, named York Street, which joined the turnpike to make a through road. We know it nowadays as Cheetham Hill Road which, winding and turning northwards from Elizabeth Street, follows the line of the old road. But looking townwards from Elizabeth Street, Cheetham Hill Road is a direct, broad thoroughfare, a tribute to the foresight of its planners.

The Half Way House has been a landmark for over a century but the building shown was demolished and replaced by the present hotel over 50 years ago

Soon after the completion of York Street, it was evident that it was going to be only a partial solution to the traffic problem. According to Partington in "Toll Bars of Manchester":

"Since 1821 the town rapidly increased and new avenues to the suburbs were loudly called for. The first project was Bury New Road from Broughton Lane to Kersal and then Prestwich and Besses. These places were previously approached by Cheetham Hill. The road to Kersal was until then a broken path through the fields."

Strangeways Lane, in pleasant countryside with the Hall on one side and meadows and a well known bowling green on the river banks, finished near Broughton Lane. From here to Broom Lane there was no defined road, merely a track over rough ground known as Stony Knolls. Streams, long since lost or built over, crossed this track and there was only an occasional cottage in sight all the way. Centuries earlier this had been part of the Roman road leading to Ribchester, but it had long since disappeared, except for short stretches at irregular intervals. In 1826 a Bill was presented to Parliament, proposing a turnpike with toll bars at Strangeways, Kersal and Besses. The road was opened in 1831 and the way was clear for increasing commercial traffic and, to borrow a phrase from a very different context, the wagons rolled!

Improved access made Broughton and Cheetham increasingly desirable places to live in and, because they attracted very little industry and had no smoky mill chimneys, they were also very healthy places. The Bleakley works at Sedgley Park had been founded in 1819 and survived until the 1970's; there were other bleach works in parts of Prestwich but the dark, satanic mills never made an appearance and the factories which filled the inner areas later in the century were unheard of at this period. People from the crowded town centres used the nearby countryside for recreation on Sundays and summer evenings and a favourite place was the Grove Inn and Pleasure Gardens. The advertisements of the period described the idyllic beauty of these gardens and offer tea in the open air, firework displays on special occasions and the excellent bowling green. We read of other tea gardens in what we would think of as unlikely areas such as Cheetwood and Rydal Mount – places which remained untouched for many years.

Perhaps the most surprising development of the period was the opening in 1838 of a Zoological Garden in Higher Broughton, between Broom Lane and Northumberland Street on a site of several acres leased from the Clowes Estate. A company of businessmen was formed to finance this venture, a collection of animals was assembled and exhibited in landscaped surroundings and the delights of a day out at this pleasure resort were advertised. Unfortunately it was not a success and after losing most of the capital they had invested, the directors gave up the venture in 1842 and sold the animals. According to some reports, many of these were bought by John Jennison, who at the time was starting a zoo on the other side of Manchester, at Belle Vue.

In addition to facilitating the movement of the increasing commercial traffic, road building encouraged house building on a scale hitherto unknown outside the growing manufacturing towns. The wealthiest merchants purchased large plots in Higher Broughton and built their own mansions, while terraces appeared along parts of Bury New Road, York Street and Broughton Lane. New streets of smaller terraces with back yards were built in the Red Bank area, including Stocks Street and Stanley Street. By the time the Ordnance Survey was conducted in 1844/6 much development had taken place and the population was rising rapidly. Although only a small part of the area had been built upon and there were very large stretches of

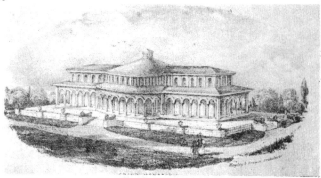

The "Grand Menagerie", Broughton Zoo, c1840

fields and farms, Broughton and Cheetham were no longer a series of quiet hamlets but an organised community. Although adjacent, they were still two communities and Cheetham opted to join Manchester in 1838 when Manchester received a charter of incorporation and elected councillors. Broughton preferred to remain a township, partly under the Lord of the Manor, for several years afterwards. But both had many public spirited men of firm religious convictions and several churches were built. The two largest and most magnificent churches of this period were St Luke's, Cheetham, and St John the Evangelist, Broughton, both consecrated in 1839 and both well known landmarks ever since. It is very sad that St Luke's is now in the course of demolition.

St Luke's was built by public subscription at a cost of £23,000, the site having been given by the Earl of Derby. The architect was T W Atkinson. At its consecration a most interesting group of local notables gathered, among whom were Chancellor Raikes and Canon Parkinson, Edward Loyd, the Banker of Greenhill, and his neighbour at Elm Bank, John Chippindall, a calico printer who reportedly contributed £1,000 towards the cost of the church. The Rev John Chippindall, his son, was Rector for nearly 40 years. Also present were Robert Garnett of Oak Hill, Halliwell Lane, and Gilbert Winter of Stocks House. The latter was one of the best known Manchester men of his day; as Boroughreeve in 1822 and then as a friend of the Stephensons, the railway pioneers. His home was open house to many of the leading men of literature, notably Charles Dickens, who met the Grant brothers at Gilbert Winter's table. Dickens based his Cheeryble brothers on these two men.

If we study the map published by the Ordnance Survey in 1848 we can see what progress had been made. Strangeways was no longer countryside and there were terraces of houses on both sides of the road as far as Strangeways Hall (now the site of the prison). Little further building had taken place along the main road until development started again at Teneriffe Street. From here to Wellington Street, large terraces with long front gardens had been built on both sides of the road and they survived until recent times. One, Belmont, has been preserved and reminds us of more than a century of Higher Broughton's history. Continuing along Bury New Road there were mansions in their own grounds on both sides of the road and down Radford Street and Vine Street. A small stretch of the newly built Great Clowes Street is shown opposite Albert Park, and Camp Street/Broughton Lane also had large terraced houses with gardens. All along Lower Broughton Road we see an irregular pattern of terraces and houses and some of the best of these, near the Cliff, are happily preserved to this day. The residents of all these newly built properties were indeed the lucky ones, combining modern (for the period) living with good, clean air and open space. Louis M Hayes tells us what it was like to move from town to Teneriffe Street at this time:

"In Manchester, about the year 1840 onwards, the middle classes began to realise that town life was

not very desirable, and families began migrating and settling in the various suburbs. In the summer of 1845 we removed from Faulkner Street to Teneriffe Street, Broughton, and it was very pleasant to get away from the town with all its dingy and uninviting surroundings, and to breathe the pure fresh, country air. The country began at this time about Sherbourne Street, fields being on both sides of the road, and as you walked along and turned down Broughton Lane it was very sweet and nice, and you realised that you had said good-bye to the town. The lane had its hedgerows thick with hawthorns and wild flowers peeping out from beneath in gay profusion, whilst the gardens about were gay with bloom. A few yards down the lane you came to Lodge's Nursery Gardens, approached by a long, wide pathway, and bordered by a small, running brook. Inside the Nurseries there was an extensive orchard of pear, apple and plum trees. Scattered about were summer houses and arbours, where people could sit and have their tea, with water-cress. In the Spring-time it was quite a sight to stand on the high ground in Bury New Road, and look across towards Lodge's Gardens, at the wide expanse of fruit trees laden with bloom. Now this ground is covered with workshops and ugly looking buildings of all descriptions.

On the other side of Broughton Lane there used to be a Racquet Court, supported principally by the German community. Amongst its members I call to mind, Milner Van Hees and his brother; Rolfsen, Stullmann and Hermes. Near to this, on the same side, stood Slade's School, afterwards occupied by Robert Neill, senior, as a private house; then by the sons, who divided it into two, and later still it became a part of their large business premises, and is so to this day.

Teneriffe Street, when we first lived there, had houses built only on one side of it, and terminated in a cul-de-sac with fields beyond. In front of the houses was a long stretch of meadowland right across to Broughton Lane. Even Great Clowes Street at this time was in its infancy, for I remember when the removal took place one of the lurries laden with furniture stuck fast in the ruts, as Great Clowes Street was then very much of a quagmire in wet weather. What happy days have I spent in and around our Teneriffe Street home!"

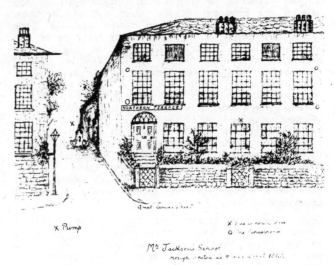

This sketch appears in the recollections of Louis M Hayes, who attended the school. Afterwards, Northern Terrace became separate large houses, numbered 182-196 Great Clowes Street and some are still standing, although they have been warehouses for many years

Broughton had indeed grown rapidly as a very high class residential suburb under the guidance of Rev J Clowes, Lord of the Manor and owner of all the land. He planned development by selling plots for "country houses" to individual buyers in selected areas from Northumberland Street northwards, and to the builders for good class terraces towards town and in the Broughton Lane area. All the land was sold subject to chief rents and the Clowes Estate grew very rich. As early as 1837 the annual income was reported to be £10,000, and this was when development was in its early stages. Ten years later a great row broke out when it was proposed that Broughton should amalgamate with Salford. Many of the local residents believed they were far superior to the Salfordians and even the Mancunians, although they usually had their businesses and earned their livings in Manchester and Salford. Views expressed were that: *"We do not wish to assimilate the cotton of Manchester or the filth of Salford"* and *"One day Broughton will be big enough to have its own Corporation."* Colonel W L Clowes, who succeeded his brother, Rev J Clowes, as Lord of the Manor, described his domain thus in 1850:

"Broughton has become a suburb of Manchester and Salford and the houses erected here are generally of a superior class. There are many villa residences, detached houses and terraces. There are few poor in the township and no common lodging houses. The land has principally been let in large plots for houses of a superior class with wide streets, well paved and generally the houses are detached and have gardens or grass plots front and back."

By 1853 agreement was reached and Broughton became part of the municipal Borough of Salford and elected its own councillors. A Broughton District Committee of the Salford Council was formed and a local Town Hall was built and opened in 1854 to facilitate administration and rate payments.

On Cheetham Hill Road the main increase in building was on the Village, from Halliwell Lane to George Street. This area has always been known as the Village from as early as 1820 and possibly earlier. The 1844/46 Ordnance Survey shows an area of small properties on either side of the main road with some larger properties nearer to Middleton Road, the most interesting of these being Wilton Polygon, some dozen large houses grouped round a central lawn and shrubbery. The entrance to this experimental development is still preserved

Teneriffe Street, "in the country" in 1845. This photograph was taken in 1932, when there were 50 people living in the two houses

as the entrance to King David School built on the site of the Polygon. At the lower end of Cheetham Hill Road, building on the newer part of York Street had begun with a few large terraces on the left hand side (from town), but the right hand side was untouched as far as the Temple. One of the largest places was Temple House, opposite St Luke's Church, which boasted a lake within its own grounds; its owner for many years was Philip Lucas. Afterwards it became a school and the site is now occupied by hundreds of terraced houses known locally as "the avenues", off Balmfield Street and Huxley Avenue. Between the two Bury Roads there was nothing but open fields. Elizabeth Street was only a track known as Dirty Lane, as was Waterloo Road, then known as Black Moor Lane. Both were adjacent to the quiet, lovely village of Cheetwood.

Great Cheetham Street had begun. The whole of Lower Broughton was empty. From Broughton Lane to the River Irwell there was still to be a few years of farmland, but Great Clowes Street had been started and was known as Broughton New Road at this point. One large, detached house stood alone for some years on a slightly elevated site. As the area was subject to flooding the house became known as Noah's Ark and is described as such on the map.

The Third Quarter 1850–1875

By 1851 the population had almost doubled in ten years, as the prospering business and professional men were attracted to the district and as their families and retinues of servants increased. Regular bus services throughout the day ran between Manchester town centre and Cheetham Hill, Higher and Lower Broughton, as well as to Prestwich, Whitefield and even as far as Bury. At the corner of Bury New Road and Knoll Street were stables for Greenwood's horses and a stopping place for their buses. The name Manchester Carriage Company is still visible on the building, commemorating the original companies which amalgamated in 1866 to operate services throughout Manchester and Salford until they, in turn, were succeeded by the Local Authorities who claimed the monopoly shortly after 1900.

The change from rural to urban areas was firmly under way by mid-century. The building industry must have been fully employed from this time onwards, as development was continuous. Cheetham Hill Road (then called York Street), from the newly erected Victoria Station, was built up as far as Elizabeth Street. By 1862 some prominent buildings, which are still standing, had been completed, notably the Cheetham Town Hall, Prestwich Union Offices, the Knowsley Hotel and the Great Synagogue. Dirty Lane disappeared and in its stead Elizabeth Street, a development of roomy family houses, appeared and found tenants immediately, many of them city merchants newly arrived from the Near East. Waterloo Road was built and partly developed, becoming the site of a plan by a forward-looking businessman, Daniel Percival, to build streets of houses for artisans in this still very desirable area. In 1857, with the help of his friends Bishop and Hewitt, Hightown was built and the first three streets were given their own names. But when this type of property was seen to have great potential, many more such streets were built. Possibly to give the district the aura of what in our own century is known as a "garden suburb", all these streets were given the names of trees. Hence Beech Street, Maple Street, Cedar Street and the others. At this time, too, Red Bank and Strangeways became crowded as the builders covered every inch of ground and the first workshops and factories appeared there.

Apart from those working on their own doorsteps, a large number of the working people who were attracted to live here at this time would have been employed in the newly erected large warehouses in the city centre. The well-known businesses of S & J Watts, J & N Philips, A & S Henry, Henry Bannerman and others were very large employers of white collar workers who laboured long hours for low wages but regarded their jobs as steadier than mill work. The proximity of Cheetham, Hightown and other new suburbs appealed to these people even when it meant a longer walk to work. This was preferable to living in the inner but more squalid areas.

Vast development of estates of terraced cottages for workers marked the third quarter of the nineteenth century. In Lower Broughton the large houses in Broughton Lane and along the new Great Clowes Street from Broughton Bridge had been rather isolated and surrounded by farms and fields, while the river still ran fairly clean and clear. By the 1860's the pattern was changing and large scale building changed the landscape completely. The 1871 Education Plan map shows that there were already schools in Duke Street, Sussex Street and Edward Street, indicating a substantial population, and within a few years Lower Broughton was completely built up with working class property and the factories and workshops which provided employment.

The Irwell floods were always an unhappy feature of life in Lower Broughton and Strangeways and; until extensive control measures were taken in recent times, very little effort was made to protect these areas. This may account for Lower Broughton remaining undeveloped for so long. However, after Broughton became part of Salford its hundreds of acres adjacent to the overcrowded slums became the "overspill" estate. Despite almost annual innundations, and a particularly disastrous flood in 1866, the builders threw up endless rows of cottages in the 1860's and 1870's until the entire area between the River Irwell, the Cheetham boundary and Broughton Lane was fully built upon.

Development northwards, beyond Broughton Lane, came later; along the recently constructed Great Clowes Street some larger houses were built and in 1877 Albert Park was opened. The Master Planner, Captain Clowes, always controlled the type of property that was built on the land he conveyed to builders by tight covenants and by reserving chief rents. Not only did he exclude many trades and severely restrict others, particularly the sale of beer and spirits, but often the minimum rateable value of houses was stipulated. The whole of what was known as Broughton Estate, from Kersal to the bottom end of Great Clowes Street, was subject to his own ideas of town planning. Thus the part of the estate nearest Manchester, being close to the river and subject to flood, was not so good a class as in the part north of Broughton Lane, according to a Manchester Guardian report. It appears that Broughton Lane should have been the edge of Lower Broughton, while the area from here to Camp Street was to contain a better class of property, leading to Higher Broughton. The higher up the hill, the higher up the social ladder and so the prominent and wealthy made their homes in Higher Broughton.

Great Cheetham Street, too, had been extended east and west. From Bury New Road to St James Road and extending to Devonshire Street, rows of identical terraced cottages in parallel streets had been built to meet the growing housing demands. Similar property had also been built from 1850 in the George Street/Thomas Street area, of what was then called Tetlow, close to the Cheetham Hill border with Broughton.

Strangeways had been gradually built up as an overflow of the town centre, and by 1860 was densely populated from the main road to the river, while Strangeways Hall with its Park had been unoccupied for a long time. When Manchester became an Assize town, a site for the new Assize Courts had to be found. Around the same time the New Bailey Prison was due for replacement and, having no further use, the ancient Hall was demolished and the magnificent Assize Courts were erected in its place and opened in 1864. Shortly afterwards the Prison was built, a grim fortress housing far more convicts today than was ever intended.

Amendments to the Poor Law encouraged the union of adjoining districts to provide better administration and larger workhouses. The Victorian attitude to the poor and the aged sick is well known. While the working classes tried to assist their own, those who had made most progress in life considered people who could not maintain themselves something of a nuisance, to be looked after as cheaply as possible. The union of North Manchester districts with Prestwich resulted in the building of Crumpsall Workhouse in 1867 to serve a much wider area than usual more economically. The continued rapid growth of the inner areas of Cheetham and Broughton obliterated any remaining dividing lines with Manchester and Salford. Only the River Irwell separated the new working populations and factories of Broughton from those of Salford, but there was not even so tangible a division between Cheetham and Manchester. Those born in the first quarter of the nineteenth century in these areas and still living at the end of the third quarter had lived through such great environmental changes that their grandchildren probably disbelieved their descriptions of their early days. The open countryside of the 1820's was a solid mass of bricks and mortar by the 1870's and building was still going on. The Inner City had been established, in some cases round the almost stately homes of the early residents in Broughton Lane and nearby. One immediate result of this was a further move outward, leading to the opening up of two of the great residential parks - Broughton Park and Sedgley Park. Both these large areas had remained the private grounds of the tenants of their respective Halls for over a century, but once they became available for development it took only a few years to create semi-private parks for the merchants and professional men of the surrounding industrial towns.

As the population swelled and the town's grip extended, a new pattern of shopping for daily needs evolved. No longer was it necessary to go to Market for whatever was not grown or produced nearby; corner shops opened in the narrow, crowded streets as soon as they were built. Very soon even the main roads became centres for shopping and some of the older terraces of large houses found their long front gardens ideal for the building of shops. On Bury Old Road a perfect example of this type of development is busier today than at any time in its long history. Union Terrace, a row of tall, Georgian houses opposite the new Cheetham Shopping Precinct, can still be seen behind the parade of shops which bears the name and accommodates many different trades. A writer in the "City Lantern" in 1876 is obviously referring to these very houses when he comments:

"Even on the main street or highway there are still rows of well-built, comfortable dwelling-houses, although, singular enough, a portion of the western side of the village is in Kersal Ward, and incorporated with the Borough of Salford. On this side of the road many of the dwelling houses have of late years been converted into shops. Not so long since, one small haberdasher's shop, one or two grocers, one or two butchers, a druggist, a greengrocer and a blacksmith, were sufficient to supply the wants of the inhabitants, and those gentry who wanted other than the most staple commodities were obliged to go to town for them. Now, however, trade is finding its level, and the

Manor Heath, Bury New Road, pictured in 1932, was typical of the mansions built in the mid-nineteenth century by the prosperous merchants and millowners

dwellers in Cheetham Hill and the vicinity can do most of their necessary shopping without being obliged to make a journey to Manchester in order to provide themselves with the necessities of life. Fishmongers, poulterers, fruiterers, newsvendors, drapers, pastry-cooks, confectioners and ironmongers have sprung up. Who knows, how soon those kindred spirits - products of modern civilisation, and equally useful in their way - the pawnbroker and the banker may appear?"

His prophecy of the arrival of the banker has been amply fulfilled, as there are now many banks and building societies among the other businesses.

Broughton Market Place was the name given to a row of well-kept shops on the site of today's Newbury Place, where Bury New Road meets Northumberland Street. The wide pavement in front of these shops could have accommodated market stalls but there is no record of any market ever being held there either before these shops were built or afterwards. Indeed, such was the character of Higher Broughton that an open-air market would have been quite unacceptable to its residents and the purpose of the wide pavement, equal in depth to the adjoining gardens, might well have been for the convenience of the carriages of the shops' customers. Until 1873 the site was open fields, although there was an unbroken line of substantial terraced houses in the direction of Manchester and mansions towards Kersal. The first six shops were soon followed by others over the next few years, following the building line and similar in design of roof and frontage to the houses. They were, however, purpose-built as shops and therefore lacked front gardens. Market Place remained a high class suburban shopping parade until the 1930's. Two names appear to have been involved in the same businesses in 1884 and 1934: the Dearnalys, butchers, and Abbey, fruiterers.

The Clowes family, as Lords of the Manor of Broughton, lived in Broughton Old Hall until about 1853 and would not sell any of the land within their personal boundaries for building. Broughton Park extended along today's Singleton Road, Park Lane, Bury New Road, Broom Lane, Leicester Road and Bury Old Road back to Singleton Road, with lodges and gates at the entrances and only the Old Hall and the New Hall within the boundaries. Beautiful homes had been built earlier in the century along Bury New Road from the Cliff on the west side and along the river banks. Between 1840 and 1850 near Kersal Bar, on the opposite side of the road, one side of Singleton Road and Park Lane also attracted individually designed mansions

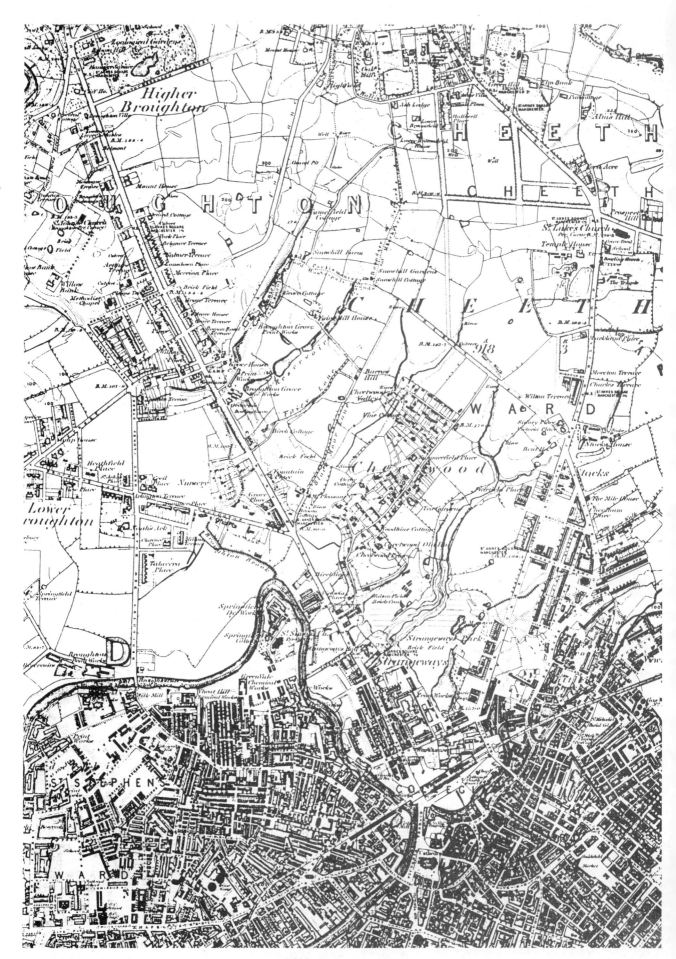

1848 Ordnance Survey

Cheetham and Broughton resurveyed in 1889, showing the inner areas of Lower Broughton, Strangeways and Red Bank solidly built-up and Hightown a little further away

with large grounds. So, too, did the Broom Lane/ Northumberland Street site of the ill-fated zoo, until eventually the Park was surrounded by high class properties . Then the Clowes Estate, who had masterminded the development of their Broughton lands, judged the time ripe for another sale of building plots. This time it was the Park itself and it must have been an event greatly and eagerly awaited at this high tide of Victorian prosperity.

The two Halls within the Park were tenanted by very prominent citizens, but their gardens were now restricted to a few acres, although the lake remained as it does to this day. New roads were built for access, but they were private roads closed by gates, with entrance greatly restricted. Upper Park Road started at the lodge in Bury Old Road, as the carriage drive had done, but its route ran roughly parallel to Bury Old Road and Singleton Road, while Waterpark Road, Old Hall Road and New Hall Road were specially built as part of the plan. The road names Old Hall and New Hall were obvious choices, but Waterpark Road was not a reference to the lake or streams in the Park. It was a compliment by Captain S W Clowes MP to his father-in-law, the third Lord Waterpark, when he married the Honourable Adelaide Cavendish in 1863.

Captain Samuel William Clowes may have lived in Broughton as a young man but this is uncertain. His home, when he succeeded his father Colonel W L Clowes in 1862, was in Leicestershire where he was a landowner, cavalry officer and Member of Parliament. But his Broughton estates were very lucrative and under his direction the Park was divided into building plots of between one and three acres and these were sold individually, subject to chief rents of around £35 an acre. He imposed the strictest covenants on the purchasers, restricting the use of the land in every way consistent with his aim of creating a most exclusive residential district. He stipulated the size of property that could be built, setting a letting value of not less than £80 per year, and on a large site fronting the newly-built Upper Park Road he called for the first house to be built at a value of £200 per year. No public house or any other type of retail business was to be allowed and all industrial premises were forbidden. The Clowes family devotion to the Established Church prompted clauses against the erection of any place of worship other than those of the Church of England. Despite these restrictions, the land was much sought after, although it is doubtful whether the privilege granted to all

tenants of the properties to be built here – that of free tolls at Broughton Bridge – was considered a great advantage!

It is probable that Woodleigh, a mansion still standing near the junction of Bury Old Road and Upper Park Road, was the first house built in Broughton Park and together with Atlow Mount and Parkfield it appears in the 1869 directory. Within a few years, Bury Old Road was lined with mansions as far as Singleton Road, while Upper Park Road and New Hall Road (from Bury New Road) were well on the way to completion. The plans of the Lord of the Manor were successfully accomplished and before the last decade of the century a new Broughton Park had arisen. Ironically, though, the Halls themselves did not survive long and by the turn of the century both the New and the Old Halls were untenanted and subsequently demolished.

The Broughton Halls and their Residents

The first three members of the Clowes dynasty to occupy Broughton Old Hall were all named Samuel and were father, son and great-grandson, the last two serving terms as High Sheriff. When the third Samuel Clowes died in 1811, aged 36, he left no son and was succeeded by his brother John, a fellow of the Collegiate Church. The development of Broughton as a high class suburb owes much to the way he controlled his sales of land to the builders and the rich men who built their own villas. In the course of these sales, on which he reserved chief rents, he became very rich. During his Lordship of the Manor, no small properties were built anywhere in Broughton and his influence in the class of property permitted to be built is shown by the fact that along Bury New Road only large houses with front and rear gardens were allowed. After his death in 1846, an entirely different type of property was built where Bury New Road ran from the Grove Inn to Strangeways; much smaller and mainly without gardens. This was, of course, outside the Clowes estates and the contrast was very noticeable, particularly as most of these houses soon became shops.

Rev John Clowes had two distant cousins of the same name, both very active in the Church, but he was more of a businessman and a socialite. He was prominent in local activities and leading members of Broughton and Cheetham Society – and, indeed, most of Manchester and Salford society – would look up to him almost as much as they did to the Earl of Wilton at Heaton Hall. One of his monuments is St John's Church, off Wellington Street, Higher Broughton. He was a generous benefactor to the foundation and he was eventually interred there. Among his many interests, it was his orchid collection which brought him country-wide renown. He employed botanists to bring him specimens from all over the world and he pioneered the culture of many splendid strains. In his Will he left the entire collection to Kew Gardens and the transfer from Broughton to London was undertaken by the leading horticulturist of the day, Sir W Hooker FRS, President of the Royal Botanical Gardens. It was recorded at the time that the Clowes Collection was unequalled even by Chatsworth or Sion House. The Reverend John Clowes died a bachelor and the heir to the estate was another brother, Colonel William Legh Clowes. It was Colonel Clowes who, in 1850, headed the petition to the Board of Health for the setting up of a local Board, a move which led to the amalgamation with Salford in 1853. His great interest when he came to Broughton in 1846 was to found a Church on Kersal Moor, " for the benefit of the poor of Rainscow." (Rainsough) This idea

The gates at the entrances to Broughton Park are remembered by older residents. This picture, taken at the corner of Waterpark Road and Broom Lane, was taken in 1928

culminated in the building of St Paul's Church in 1851-2. Horse racing on Kersal Moor had recently ceased and the grandstand, owned by the Colonel, was licensed to be used as a church in the years before St Paul's opened. The land was donated jointly by Colonel Clowes and Miss Atherton of Kersal Cell and, together with their families, they also gave £1,600 to the building fund.

Broughton Old Hall remained empty for some years after Colonel W L Clowes left the district but in 1864 a tenant was found. Henry Davis Pochin was a man of many parts. A successful industrialist, he was also an active member of the Salford Borough Council from 1854 until he moved to London about 1869, after serving as Mayor for two successive years. As a loyal member of the Council, it is remarkable that he should be sympathetic towards women's suffrage, as a letter dated 2nd March 1868, headed "Broughton Old Hall, Manchester", shows. (He includes Broughton in Manchester, although as an Alderman he certainly knew it was in Salford!) "Votes for Women!" was a strident call forty years later and took many years and a Great War to come to fruition, so we don't expect rich Victorian businessmen to be in the forefront of the movement:

"To the Overseers of the Broughton District.

Gentlemen,
Allow me to call your attention to the following facts which in the opinion of many eminent legal minds entitle women to be placed on the register of voters for Members of Parliament if they have the qualification which in the case of men would entitle them to be so placed.

The Legislation in the Representation of the People Act 1867 has discarded the word 'Male persons' employed in the Reform Act of 1832 to indicate those on whom the franchises created by that Act were conferred and in place thereof has substituted the generic term 'man' which has a wider signification than that of 'adult male' for instance in the legal sense....If you coincide with this view of the matter, you will of course place qualified women on the Register and I shall be obliged by your attention to the points here submitted.

I am, Gentlemen, Yours very respectfully,
Henry D Pochin

The reply came that the Overseers could not place women on the List of Voters and they suggested that *"the better course would be that each woman who is considered qualified, should make a claim to be put in the Register to be sent to the Overseers."*

The Alderman's interest becomes apparent in a letter of a few days later:

"Broughton Old Hall
Manchester
July 21st

To the Overseers of Broughton

Gentlemen,
In order to carry out your suggestion in your letter of the 18th in reference to the claims of qualified women to be placed on the register we should be obliged if you would give us from the Rate Book the names and addresses of the female householders who have paid the suffrage rate and all other rates levied upon them. Or if you cannot do this, will you be good enough to allow us such facilities as will enable us to do it for ourselves by allowing a person authorized by us for that purpose access to the Books?

An answer will oblige.

Yours very respectfully,
Agnes Pochin, on behalf of the National Society for the promotion of Womens' Suffrage

Henry Pochin was obviously an attentive husband who wanted to help his wife's good cause. Regrettably, the efforts of the Pochins were defeated by bureaucratic difficulties.

The New Hall had served illustrious tenants in the course of the nineteenth century, the first one recorded being William Jones, the banker, who, in partnership with his brother and Edward Loyd, traded as Jones Loyd in King Street. He died in 1821 and for the next seven years the New Hall was occupied by James Hibbert, a magistrate and export merchant who traded with Europe until Napoleon's blockade of British shipping. To avoid this, he traded with Portugal and in 1808 sailed for Brazil to open a branch of his business in Rio de Janeiro. He was typical of the early Manchester merchants, having started his business in 1788 by travelling through England on horseback, seeking customers in every town and village.

For 30 years from 1832, James C Harter lived in great style at the New Hall. He played host to Mr Gladstone, then Chancellor of the Exchequer, when he visited Manchester and Salford in 1853. Mr Harter was for many years Treasurer of the Royal Infirmary and very active in charitable and local affairs. Between 1873 and 1884 the New Hall was tenanted by Julius Steinberg, a merchant in the firm of Paul and Steinberg and a native of Germany. He had lived in Hanover Square, Bury New Road, since 1851.

From about 1870 the tenant of the Old Hall was James Bancroft Esquire, which is how he was described in the directories of the time and earlier when he lived at Noah's Ark, the elevated mansion in Great Clowes Street. This courtesy title appears after no other name in Broughton Park. His co-tenant at Noah's Ark was William Southern, a builder who became his neighbour in the newly-erected Rookswood, adjacent to the Old Hall. In 1872 James Bancroft persuaded the trustees of the Clowes Estate to allow the building of the Congregational Church in Upper Park Road (which is still in use), despite their objections to a Nonconformist place of worship in Broughton Park. The builders were W Southern and Son and James Bancroft laid the foundation stone. These two gentlemen were probably closely related as the census of 1861 shows William Southern, a builder, living in Camp Street with a five year old son named James Bancroft Southern.

The development of Sedgley Park as a residential retreat for the merchant princes was concurrent with the progress of Broughton Park. The 1844/6 Ordnance Survey had shown only Woodhill and Sedgley Hall south of Scholes Lane between the two Bury roads, with such landmarks as Hilton House (Hall), Barnfield, Butt Hill, High Bank, Singleton (Brooklands) and Singleton Lodge as their neighbours. The last named stood on Castle Hill, thought to be the site of a Roman camp, near Singleton Road, and was the home of the Wood family for almost a century. George William Wood (1781-1843) was a Member of Parliament, a magistrate, President of the Chamber of Commerce and a leading figure in Manchester. His son, W Rayner Wood, was also very prominent in his day. Within 20 years the Old Hall had been joined by a New Hall as well as a magnificent row of mansions on both sides of Sedgley Park Road and Bent Hill (later Prestwich Town Hall) on Scholes Lane. Henry Tootal Broadhurst and his partner Henry Lee JP, of the famous textile firm, lived here, as did Henry Bannerman of similar fame.

The mid-Victorian years of Manchester's prosperity produced another generation of solid businessmen whose long working day required a home within driving distance of the office or mill. Broughton Park, Kersal and Prestwich were ideally situated for them and gradually these areas, particularly on the Bury New Road side, were linked up. The period 1860-1880 witnessed the building of many houses near Moor Lane, along Singleton Road and the start of Cavendish Road. Some of these survive, notably the Hazeldean Hotel and the George Hotel in Sedgley Park.

The dominant position in world trade held by Manchester attracted businessmen from Europe and the Mediterranean to establish branches here and so be close to the source of supply. In Higher Broughton by mid-century there were many prosperous merchants in Northumberland Street and nearby who had been born in the Ottoman Empire. These men settled and brought up their families here and their presence and success brought others to join them. By 1860 they founded their own Church, the magnificent Greek Church on Bury New Road, which is still in use.

One of the best known of the Greek merchants was Sotiris Hazzopulo, who was born in Constantinople and came to Manchester to trade in yarn with Turkey, Greece and Persia. On one occasion he entertained Crown Prince Constantine at his residence, Bella Vista, on Bury New Road. While he was Consul General for Persia he attended upon the Shah, who came to Manchester during a State Visit.

The permanent residence for the Bishop of Manchester, Bishopscourt, was built at Higher Broughton and has remained, after major alterations, for over a century. The Deanery was built immediately across Bury New Road at the corner of Park Lane, on the site of the home of Alderman Willert, one of the leaders of the Manchester Council for over a generation. Many other Aldermen and former Mayors resided in the area, including Alderman Neill, who lived at Midfield, Northumberland Street, and who, after two terms as Mayor of Manchester, laid the foundation stone of the present Town Hall. Joseph Heron (later Sir Joseph), although Town Clerk of Manchester, lived for many years on Bury New Road opposite Devonshire Street before moving to Broughton Park. Her Majesty's Justices have lodged in Vine Street when at Manchester Assizes ever since those days. Cheetham Hill, too, attracted prominent characters in public life, including Alderman Grave, who was Mayor no fewer than three times, and the name of Councillor Muirhead, if not remembered for his civic duties, reminds us of the well-known fishmongers.

Broughton becomes part of Salford 1847–53

Although Broughton has been part of the City and Borough of Salford for well over a century, most of its residents tend to think of Salford as a different and even somewhat distant place. They know they are its citizens, ratepayers and voters, but Salford's unfortunate lack of a city centre must be one cause of this feeling of not really belonging. The union of Broughton with the Borough of Salford was agreed in 1853 but was preceded by several years of controversy, mostly centred around the argument that there was little affinity between the two places.

Broughton had only 880 inhabitants in 1821, but 20 years later there were 3,800. The population increased rapidly to reach over 5,000 by 1847, when the pace of progress was causing problems. Sanitation was very little better than it had been a quarter of a century earlier, but Parliament had, in recent years, been roused to demand higher standards in Public Health and the incorporated boroughs with salaried staffs were building sewers and providing purer water supplies. This led a group of Broughton ratepayers to approach the Salford Council for a union to provide them with the means of giving their township good sanitation, lighting and watch (police) services. The idea of an amalgamation made an instant appeal to Salford and they very quickly laid plans to promote an Act of Parliament to bring Pendleton (which had made no approach) and Broughton, both already in the Parliamentary Borough, into the Municipal boundaries.

The Broughton residents who had made the approach overestimated the support they would receive and the newspaper correspondence of the ensuing weeks shows great hostility. Indeed, some people thought that Broughton would derive greater advantage from incorporation with Manchester, since it adjoined Cheetham but was separated from Salford by the Irwell, over which there was at this time only one bridge. Many of the merchants, factory owners, shippers, bankers, agents and members of the professions who had settled in Broughton had lived in the town centres, either on or near to their places of business, and they announced that they wished to have no association with their former neighbours or workpeople. One speaker at a ratepayers' meeting at the Griffin Hotel described Manchester and Salford working people and their surroundings in so insulting a manner that he was obliged to write a long letter to the Manchester Guardian explaining in detail why he believed that Manchester and Salford were places of business and Broughton was a place of residence and therefore required a different form of local government. He was unrepentant about his views on the undesirability of amalgamating this very superior suburb with the industrialised and densely populated town. The Manchester Guardian commented:

"We allude to the desire among men who are or have been engaged in trade in Manchester or Salford whose property is benefitted and increased in value by the exercise of its industry to withdraw their services and the fair contribution of their property from the government and protection of the community to which they owe their success."

Opposition to the amalgamation was strong enough to prevent any progress and no further action took place until 1850 when, following a petition by Colonel W L Clowes and 139 other ratepayers to the General Board of Health in London, an Inquiry under the Public Health Act of 1848 was held by Robert Rawlinson, the Superintending Inspector. His mission was to inquire publicly into Broughton's sewerage, drainage, water supply and sanitary conditions, as well as matters of paving, lighting, cleansing and watching, in all of which the petitioners knew that great improvements were essential.

The Rawlinson report praised Broughton in many ways. It referred to a low mortality rate, absence of fever and that the land was laid out on a most liberal scale. Evidence was given that Broughton had no masses of people congregated together in crowded and ill-ventilated dwellings, half-clothed, poorly-fed and worse housed. If only Engels had described Broughton instead of Manchester!

The report concluded that the means of sewerage, drainage and water supply were "imperfect" and that Broughton should take remedial action jointly with the larger authorities and that in order to conduct the township's affairs for the future a local Board of Health should be elected with the necessary powers. Although arrangements were, in fact, made to set up such a Board, the scheme was dropped in 1851 and the issue of amalgamation with Salford was revived with very influential support following a Rawlinson Report on Pendleton. Referring to the proposal to extend the Salford boundaries to include Pendleton and Broughton, Mr Rawlinson commented that: *"such an extension would be to the greatest possible advantage to the inhabitants of both these districts."*

Joseph Brotherton had been Member of Parliament for Salford, Broughton and Pendleton since 1832. He was very active locally and greatly respected, and when he heard that Rawlinson favoured the amalgamation as the means of better local government, he set out to achieve it. Accordingly, he

BROUGHTON.

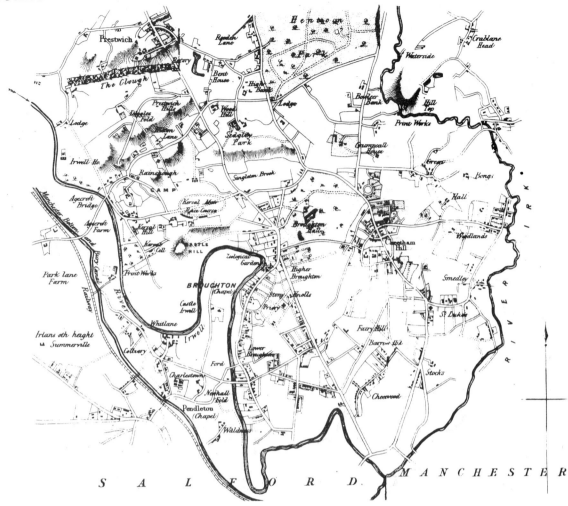

This map of 1850 shows Broughton and Cheetham Hill together with the surrounding districts of Pendleton, Prestwich and Crumpsall

approached the local officers of both townships in separate meetings and suggested terms which included very generous representation on an augmented Salford Town Council. The latter were once again most co—operative, offering the districts very large measures of autonomy, but the Broughton opposition was still very active and at a public meeting early in 1852 the vote was only 41–29 in favour. Even when, after friendly negotiations, agreement was reached for Salford to promote a Bill in Parliament, there were still storms ahead. After the House of Commons passed a measure in 1853, the opponents took their objections to the House of Lords and forced another ballot of the ratepayers. Their Lordships' verdict favoured amalgamation and the voters of Broughton elected their own councillors for the first time in November 1853.

A Broughton District Committee was immediately constituted with several sub—committees and Broughton Town Hall was built to assist rate collection as well as administration. The District Committee continued to function for some 40 years but ultimately a unified Salford Council dissolved both districts' separate organisations and it is most unlikely that there will ever be a separatist movement in the future.

Cheetham or Cheetham Hill?

What is the correct designation of the district which follows the length of Cheetham Hill Road from Manchester to Middleton Road, and includes the industrial and residential areas on both sides of the road? Is it Cheetham or Cheetham Hill? Nowadays, "Cheetham Hill" is generally used for the whole district and we seldom hear of Cheetham except as a ward of the City Council. To old or former residents there is a distinct difference and until recently there was both a Cheetham Cricket Club and a Cheetham Hill Cricket Club. Now only the latter survives.

In recent years a new shopping precinct has been opened in Cheetham Hill village but, for some unknown reason, the developers named it Cheetham Parade; as Broughton, Crumpsall and Cheetham all meet near this point they had a wide choice of names.

"Cheetham" is derived from the Chetham family (pronounced Cheetham), who were wealthy land-owners as early as the sixteenth century. They built Crumpsall Hall, which stood in Crescent Road until 1825, and also Smedley Old Hall. Humphrey Chetham, who built and endowed the College still flourishing near the Cathedral, was born in 1580 at Crumpsall Hall. Cheetham was a township in the Parish of Manchester and extended from the Town end of Cheetham Hill Road to Crescent Road, taking in the village of Cheetham Hill. According to a correspondent in "Manchester City News Notes and Queries", at the end of a controversy in 1886:

"Cheetham Hill is a village in the township of Manchester and is distant 2 miles from St Ann's Square. Halliwell Lane is the boundary of the village as we go to it from Manchester. This is one foot of the hill. Passing onwards to the Griffin Inn and Mount College we find ourselves on

the top of the hill from which the village takes its name. From this place to the Robin Hood the descent is considerable. At a short distance beyond the Robin Hood is Boundary Street, which separates Cheetham from Broughton."

When this was written there had been extensive development in North Manchester and it was vastly different from the Cheetham and Cheetham Hill of the early part of the nineteenth century.

The Cheetham Rate Book for 1822 shows a total population of only 2,027. It is divided into districts and shows Cheetham Hill with 30 to 40 tenants, mostly in large houses, some in several acres of gardens. It shows Smedley taking in Smedley Lane, Smedley Road, some large houses and estates, two halls, some mills and a few smaller houses. Temple was the name given to half a dozen residences near Smedley Lane and Stocks comprised a stately home, estate, adjoining land and cottages. There were a few smaller houses in York Street, the newly built main road later to be known as Cheetham Hill Road, and in Strangeways there were more of these smaller properties.

The most interesting of all these districts was probably Cheetwood, an isolated country village which was a real beauty spot and could have been far away from the grime and squalor of inner Manchester. In fact, it was within one mile of the town, being the area behind Cheetham Park which later became the site of the many brickworks and, later, the factories which today cover the whole area.

Cheetham Hill was described at this time as a genteel neighbourhood and it certainly merited this description. The largest houses along the main road had been built in the last decades of the eighteenth century by the first of the wealthy merchants and manufacturers and five of their residences occupied almost the whole of one side of the road. Halliwell Lane and Tetlow Lane had a similar group of lordly mansions, as did Smedley Lane. Some twenty of the early beneficiaries of the Industrial Revolution resided in Cheetham Hill and Cheetham, enjoying a lifestyle similar to that hitherto enjoyed only by the landed gentry.

Prosperous Kersal

The boundary between Broughton and Prestwich follows the line of the Singleton Brook, nowadays a miserable ditch visible in only a few places and nobody's idea of a tinkling stream or babbling brook! We used to see it first behind Park Road; it was culverted under Bury Old Road and then ran along between Cavendish Road and Albert Avenue across Kersal Moor and emptied into the Irwell near Cussons' soap factory. On neither side of the boundary was there any residential development in the first half of the nineteenth century and so it remained open countryside.

As a thoroughfare, Singleton Road is very old indeed and before Bury New Road was built around 1830 it was continuous with Moor Lane and was the only connecting road between Bury Old Road and Bolton Road. There was a toll bar at the Bury Old Road corner and Singleton Road carried a great volume of wheeled traffic during Whit Week, or whenever the great event of the year, the Kersal Moor Races, took place.

It remained a rural area until about 1840, when the prosperous merchants and manufacturers started to build their mansions in the pleasant green fields of Higher Broughton and Kersal. The census of 1851 shows Singleton Brook House occupied by Joseph Peel, a magistrate and ironfounder, with four daughters, one son and four servants. John Wilson, a calico printer, lived at Singleton House with his wife, five children and six servants.

These two houses, each in two or three acres of land, were demolished long ago, but Park Cottage, then occupied by William H Myers, an attorney, survives to this day.

Gradually the road was built up on both sides along the whole length and by the 1880's only at Park Lane corner was there a vacant plot. Most of the houses stood in extensive grounds and in later years Limefield Road and the end of Cavendish Road were created out of their gardens and orchards. Singleton Hill, which today houses youth clubs, was occupied 100 years ago by J T Johnson, aged 45, and his wife, two children, a governess and five servants. Mr Johnson described himself as an ironmaster employing 882 people. He was a partner in Richard Johnson and Nephew, the wire manufacturers whose large works in East Manchester was very well known until its recent closure.

A landmark in Singleton Road until recent years was the Presbyterian Church, which was hit by a bomb in 1940. This had been built in 1873 by John Stuart, a banker who lived on the front of Bury New Road, opposite Vine Street, and who paid the whole cost of £7,000. Still surviving as residences are Kersal Hill, Morningside and Rock Avon, as well as Stenecourt, now the Great and New Synagogue. This was once known as Endrick Lodge, but the name was changed long ago by a previous owner. Strangely enough, one gatepost near Holden Road reads "Stenecourt", while the other reads "Lodge".

In contrast with Singleton Road, Cavendish Road, originally named Cavendish Street, was created by a few prosperous businessmen in the booming mid-Victorian era of the 1860's and 1870's. In the 1881 census there are details of the occupants of the half-dozen mansions which stood along the left hand side between Bury New Road and a cul-de-sac where Limefield Road now stands. Two of the original houses still stand, Fairhill and Grotburn, while the houses in Carmona Gardens replaced the original Carmona, home of Henry Spurrier, the oil merchant whose firm Spurrier Glazebrook still flourishes. Peter Allen, who lived at Overbrook with his son, employed a cook, four other servants and a coachman who had a cottage in the grounds. Mr Allen was described as a newspaper proprietor, and as his firm was Taylor Garnett & Company, his newspaper was none other than the Manchester Guardian. Other interesting residents of Cavendish Road a century ago were the three Woolley brothers, all pharmaceutical chemists. Their firm was James Woolley & Company, the wholesale druggists known to generations of chemists but now, I understand, merged with other, similar, firms.

Kersal Bar

When the tram stopped at the junction of Bury New Road and Moor Lane and the conductor called out, "Kersal Bar!", none of his passengers thought of liquid refreshment. We all knew the small, unusual building at the stop, which housed a newsagent's, sweets and tobacconist's shop, as "the Bar", but we had no idea of its history or significance. The single-storey, lodge-like structure with the bay window, known to many Higher Broughton and Kersal residents and passed daily by thousands of others from Prestwich and Whitefield, is 150 years old and was built as the toll house when Bury New Road was made in 1831. A gate, or bar, was erected here and travellers paid the tollkeeper to pass through.

The Turnpike Trusts built and maintained many roads throughout the country at a time when there were no Local Authorities able to provide the capital for such projects. They were profitable to the trustees, whose income steadily rose with the increase of industrial traffic. Along Bury New Road

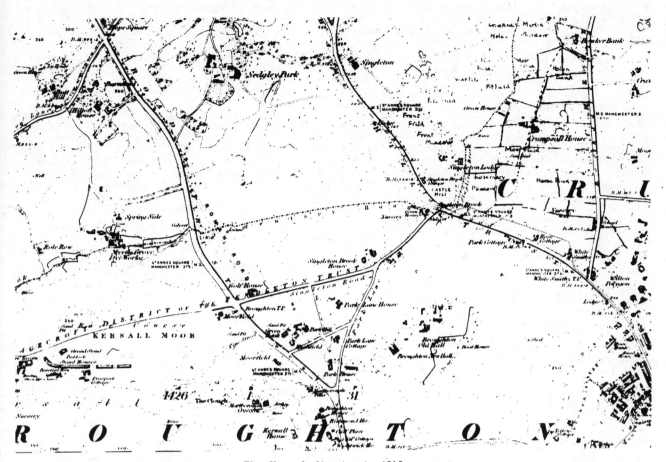

The Kersal district in 1848

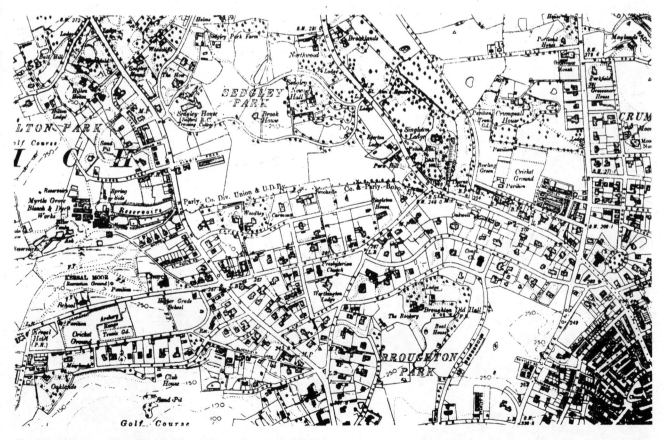

North of Broom Lane by 1910, there were mostly large houses standing in their own grounds. Only in the Thomas Street area of Cheetham Hill had there been large-scale cottage development

trundled wagons drawn by teams of powerful horses bringing cloth from the mills of Lancashire towns to the warehouses of Portland Street and Princess Street for customers all over the world.

The Kersal toll house was typical of many others long since demolished. Its window was built out so that the collector had a clear view of the road and no doubt in bad weather he had a great advantage over the traveller.

When local government became well established and public transport developed, the tolls were abolished and Bury New Road was freed. In the 1884 directory William Butterworth, who in previous issues had been described as a toll collector, was listed as a newsagent, and was similarly described in subsequent years. Was this his compensation for loss of office, an early example of the Golden Handshake? It is interesting to note that this is the only shop in an area where the landowner's restrictive covenants have prevented any form of commercial development in the last 100 years or more.

Mr Gladstone dined in Broughton Park

Although it is unlikely that anyone nowadays can remember Mr Gladstone personally, or even as a living character, his name is known to many as a great Prime Minister of the last century. His career spanned the whole of the Victorian era, he occupied 10 Downing Street several times and some of his extra-political activities are still the subject of controversy.

In 1853 he was the Chancellor of the Exchequer in Lord Aberdeen's Government and in November of that year he visited Manchester and Salford for four very busy days. For Broughton it was a very exciting time since the township of some 8,000 residents, mostly business, professional and middle class, had just amalgamated with Salford and had held its first elections to the Council.

At London Road Station Mr and Mrs Gladstone were met by James Harter jnr, son of Mr J C Harter, who had been resident at Broughton New Hall for over 20 years, and the distinguished party proceeded there in carriages. Mr Harter was a very prominent businessman of his time and must have had great influence in high places to have played host for several days to a senior Cabinet Minister. He would have had little difficulty in catering for his distinguished guests, as there were nine resident servants and no doubt some non-resident as well. The guests included the Bishop of Manchester, several other Church leaders, the Mayor of Manchester, the President of the Chamber of Commerce, the local Member of Parliament, Mr Joseph Brotherton, and many others. Regrettably, the newspapers did not publish details of the menu!

Next day Mr Gladstone visited factories and warehouses in Manchester and was again entertained to dinner in Broughton, this time at the home of Mr William Slater in Park Lane, a short distance from the Hall. Slater was an attorney and a man of some wealth; he had been one of the founders of St Paul's Church, Kersal, in 1852, and had contributed £500 to the Building Fund. The other guests included the Mayor of Salford and several local worthies.

Nothing remains of either the Old or New Halls except the roads named after them, the Park and the Lake, but in the centre of Manchester, at the rear of Portland Street, there is Harter Street, a short, narrow street which was once part of King Cotton's empire. Is this a link with a great Manchester man who entertained statesmen in his own stately home?

Kersal Moor in the news

As it was the largest and most accessible open space in the neighbourhood of Manchester, Kersal Moor attracted large crowds for public meetings on many occasions. In 1818 a coal miners' protest meeting was held there to publicise their case for

Kersal Bar. The original toll house pictured in Edwardian times is still a newsagent's shop

improved pay because of the dangers they faced in their work. They were working up to 12 hours daily for 14 shillings per week and a poster advertising the meeting thought £1 weekly not an unreasonable request.

In September 1838, a Radical movement popularly known as Chartism called a meeting of workers and politicians in favour of further franchise reforms. They called on working people within a radius of several miles to take a day off from the mills and factories to march to Kersal Moor and demonstrate in favour of votes for all men over 21, irrespective of property qualification, and other franchise and parliamentary reforms. Remembering the tragic meeting only 19 years earlier at Peterloo, the organisers, who included members of Parliament and some business people, promised the magistrates that it would be a very peaceful gathering and there were no serious incidents. They claimed that 300,000 people would attend and this figure appears in some histories as the number who assembled that day on Kersal Moor. However, it is very difficult to imagine the equivalent of three Cup Final crowds making their way to and from the Moor along the very narrow access roads of those days! The Manchester Guardian published a very detailed report of all the speeches but ridiculed the 300,000 figure; their estimate was 25,000.

In 1846 it was reported that Kersal Moor was to become an encampment for certain regiments of the army, although soldiers in this country had usually been in barracks since 1812. Apparently the War Office wished to give them the experience of service "in the tented field". In 1831 the Moor had been the scene of a review of 3,000 troops by Lord Hill.

Although horse racing on Kersal Moor took place annually for nearly two hundred years and always attracted very large crowds, the owners of the land, the Byrom and the Chetham families, were never very happy with these activities and many quarrels are recorded preceding the annual leases to the Stewards. When the Clowes succeeded the Chethams they often showed opposition to the sport and by 1846 Miss Atherton, the last of the Byroms, and Colonel Clowes finally refused to renew the lease. A newspaper report of November 1846 reads:

"We stated some time since that it was definitively decided by the joint owners of Kersal Moor that this piece of ground should no longer be used for the purpose of horse races. The determination of the proprietors of the land is about to be carried out, by the taking down of all the stands, with the exception of the grand stand. We understand that in the high wind during the night of Thursday week, two of the high brick erections, the roofs of which form the stands, while below they are fitted up as booths and bars, fell with great violence to the ground; but fortunately without the slightest personal injury to anyone. The shorter range, that nearest Manchester, is about 470 feet long, and the other is 700 feet in length. We believe that when these erections shall have disappeared, the moor is otherwise to remain in statu quo. So far as we can learn, there is no present intention of allowing it to be built upon. As the racing vocation of Kersal Moor is now a matter of history, we may state, for the information of the curious, that the length of the course is 1,636 yards, measured on the right hand or inward side, 1,681 yards, measured along the middle of the course; and 1,726 yards on the left or outward side of the course. The distance from the Exchange to the grand stand, by the new Bury Road and the carriage road across the moor, is 2 miles 7 furlongs and 192 yards - just 28 yards short of 3 miles."

Colonel Clowes soon found a new use for the grand stand, one much nearer to his heart, when he obtained the blessing of the Bishop of Manchester for its becoming a place of worship for the poor

inhabitants of Rainsough. It was very successful both as a church and as a school, where the teachers, possibly including his own daughters, were supplied by the Colonel himself.

The banker, Edward Loyd jnr, whose father had been a founder of St Luke's Church on Cheetham Hill Road, was living in Prestwich and as the Clowes and Loyd families were close friends he attended the service at the grand stand. When he asked why they did not have a church there, he was told that nothing was wanted but money. Loyd immediately offered £500 - equal to, say, £50,000 at today's value - and was soon joined by Colonel Clowes, Miss Atherton and William Slater of Park Lane with similar offers and many others joined in with generous donations. It was already decided to build a small church when Mr Robert Gladstone, whose wife had recently died, came along with a promise of £1,000 in her memory and an offer to raise more money if the sponsors would build a bigger church; one which would attract an eminent Minister. The project to build the magnificent St Paul's Church, which is still with us, went ahead and the church has prospered for well over a century.

Mr Gladstone was a merchant and agent for cotton, trading with India, China and Russia. At this time he lived at Mount House, Tetlow Fold, and although only forty years old he was a magistrate. Later he moved a short distance to Highfield, Great Cheetham Street East. In 1861 he had re-married and had five children at home, together with a butler, cook, nurse, coachman and five other servants. The site of Highfield is still marked by a plaque over some shops in Great Cheetham Street. His son, Murray Gladstone, lived at Broughton House in Bury New Road (not to be confused with Broughton House, Park Lane, the ex-Servicemen's Home), which later became the site of Bishopscourt.

Collecting the Poor Rate

In an age when the standard of living of the working people was so low, the plight of the sick, the aged and the unemployed was indeed desperate and the operation of the Poor Law provided the barest minimum of help. Funds were raised by Overseers through an early form of local rating, but collection of the monies was beset, as today, with many difficulties.

The minutes of the Broughton Overseers contain many excuses, as well as genuine reasons, for non-payment or assessment-reduction and the following are some examples...

H D Pochin was a manufacturing chemist with a large works in Salford and was obviously a wealthy man wishing to live in superb style. Nevertheless, as a keen businessman one of his first acts upon taking up residence was to appeal against his rating assessment:

"MEETING OF THE OVERSEERS OF BROUGHTON held at the Town Hall, April 28th 1865
Present: Mr C Y Robotham (in the Chair), R H Gibson, F Manginall
Memorandum: On the 11th day of February last Mr H D Pochin of Broughton Old Hall appealed to the Magistrates at petty Sessions held at the Town Hall Salford against the Gross Rental of £300 upon his House and Buildings he being satisfied with the Gross Rental of £100 for the land - being the pleasure ground gardens and 10 acres meadow land : his plea against the Assessment of the House being in excess of the Rental named in his lease viz:- £200. Mr Pochin's Lease being a repairing lease the Overseers held that £100 was required to keep the place in repair according to the terms of the lease and that £300 was a reasonable rent from year to year the Landlord to do all the repairs."

However, the magistrates decided in favour of Mr Pochin and reduced the rental to £200. The Overseers felt aggrieved at the decision and appealed to the Quarter Sessions. That court reversed the decision of the magistrates and placed the rental at £250.

"Resolved: That Cheques for the following amounts be signed to pay the Costs of the Overseers in the above named appeals

Mr Heron Solicitor	£82 4s 8d
Mr Fisher Valuer	£16 3s 0d
Mr Hewitt -do.-	£18 7s 6d
Mr Lawton -do.-	£26 18s 6d
Mr Vasavour Agent	£5 5s 0d
	£148 18s 8d

The rates at the time were around 2/6d in the £ (12½%), so that the full assessment to poor rates amounted to perhaps £40 per annum and Mr Pochin eventually saved £5 per annum. The unfortunate Overseers had to pay a bill representing several years' contributions from this ratepayer, spread, of course, over the whole township.

Mr Pochin was not alone in attempting to reduce his personal liability to the poor and the records show owner after owner of prestigious property trying to obtain reductions and often succeeding in saving themselves as much as five pounds per annum. The savings could seldom be more, since the rate in the £ was so low and, indeed, all forms of taxation at the time seem incomprehensible to us. Even Sir Joseph Heron, celebrated as the first Town Clerk of Manchester and credited with setting up most of the successful departments of the City, joined the rates appeal bandwagon as soon as he had moved into his newly-built residence, "Rookswood", in Broughton Park.

Many other rating appeals were much more deserving. In 1865 a Mrs Hufton appeared before the Overseers asking to be excused from paying her poor rates (just over £1) as she couldn't afford it. She was a widow with seven children and only one of them was working, earning just three shillings per week. Mrs Hufton was excused payment.

In 1867 Mrs Marsden, who was described as a farmer of Kersal Moor, appealed for time to pay her rates owing to a dreadful misfortune. She had lost all her cattle that year in an outbreak of cattle plague. The Overseers were sympathetic and she was allowed time to pay. Month after month very poor people had their rates excused, but the amounts usually involved were small, often less than one pound.

One of the more unusual rate reduction requests was in 1877 from Mr S Hazzopulo, the owner of Bella Vista. (Years later this building was known to generations of schoolgirls and parents as Broughton High School at the corner of Bury New Road and Broom Lane.) Mr Hazzopulo had suffered so serious a fire that only two rooms were inhabitable; one for himself and one for his servants. Although a fire might not be grounds for relief from rates, he stated that he was unable to obtain a contract for the necessary repairs as there was a joiners' strike. We do not know how long this lasted but for that year Mr Hazzopulo was somewhat consoled by being excused half the rates.

There were other problems connected with payment of rates which the Overseers had to contend with. In Lower Broughton a Mr William Matthews was landlord of the Vavasour Hotel in Sussex Street and he was also landlord to as many as 200 cottage dwellers nearby. In 1868 the assistant rates collector was threatened with violence by Matthews, whom he accused of "disturbing" his tenants by calling upon them for rates. A few years later this same William Matthews was reported for refusing to pay rates on his cottage properties when the tenants were in arrears with their rent. Landlords like Mr Matthews were allowed reduced assessments when they were responsible for paying rates, presumably to include the arrears factor, and the committee resolved *"that if he is not prepared to pay for occupied time of all his cottages over 4/9d per week, even if the tenant is in arrears, his cottages will be placed on higher assessments and rates collected from the tenants."*

A Cradle of Sport

Reference has already been made to the intense local interest in the sport of archery and the great prowess of participants living in Cheetham Hill and Broughton, which earned the admiration of large numbers of followers of the art in all parts of Manchester and further afield.

Kersal Moor Races were attended annually by many thousands of enthusiasts who invaded the area from far and wide. Even after the races were transferred to Castle Irwell in 1847, the Broughton area was still the home of horse racing. In at least two other popular sports – golf and cricket – Broughton men were pioneers.

The game of golf is, of course, of Scottish origin and was played North of the border for many a year before it was played in England. In 1814 a small group of Manchester businessmen, some of whom had emigrated from Scotland, formed a Golf Club and the first recorded round took place in 1820 on Kersal Moor. At that time the "course" consisted of only five holes and since the Moor was the natural assembly ground for so many other activities it did not boast defined fairways and closely cropped greens. Nevertheless, in the whole of England only one other club, Blackheath, played golf at this time and for some years afterwards. The surprise these local pioneers provided for onlookers must have been very real and the early members, who called themselves the Manchester Golf Club, must have been very long-suffering when we recall that race meetings, public meetings and the everyday country walks and sports of the population regularly overran these new sporting activities.

The Broughton Cricket Club has been described as one of the oldest in the world, having been founded in 1823, with a small ground on Lower Broughton Road and later on the site of Albert Park. For some years there were two cricket clubs in Broughton and the rival Athenaeum Club also attracted many members, not necessarily local residents. The present ground off Great Clowes Street has been in use for well over a century and has seen many famous characters, foremost of whom was W G Grace, who brought a South of England team to Broughton. One of the early Australian touring teams also played here in July 1880, including the original "demon bowler", Spofforth. The match was scheduled for three days, but even a hundred years ago our local weather was much the same as today, so the first day and half of the second day saw no play because of rain. The 6,000 spectators witnessed a drawn match with very low scoring, despite Broughton being allowed to play 18 men to the Australians' 11. Cheetham Hill Cricket Club, still happily prospering, was a great rival to the Broughton Club and their annual "derby" matches were the highlights of the season, as the report dated May 1871 in "The Sphinx", a magazine circulated in the Manchester area, shows. Each of the cricket clubs also had their own bowling green and so they also played each other annually at bowls.

THE SPHINX.

CRICKET

CHEETHAM HILL v BROUGHTON

The first cricket match this season between the

Cheetham Hill Club and Ground and the Broughton Club, was played last Saturday on the ground of the former at Higher Crumpsall. The arrangements of this home-and-home match allow the Cheetham Hill Club to play their professional bowlers, while Broughton relies entirely upon the amateur members of the club. Considering the result of last Saturday's match we should think that, after this season, the two clubs ought to meet each other on equal terms.

Notwithstanding the encroachments of the town upon its ancient suburbs and adjoining villages, the village of Cheetham Hill remains wonderfully homogenous, and retains many of its pristine characteristics. The inhabitants are clannish, intact and enthusiastic. Everybody appears to know everybody else, and mayors, aldermen, merchants, calico-printers, parsons, publicans and sinners seem to be all jumbled up together. No doubt this is of vast service to the Cheetham Hill Club, and accordingly the denizens of the neighbourhood, of both sexes, turn out in great numbers at their cricket matches.

The Broughton players having won the toss, were first to appear at the wickets. They did not long remain there. Mr J Makinson does not appear to like the ground, or the ground does not appear to suit him, for, if we remember correctly, last year he only scored four, and on Saturday he was bowled by Wardle for two. On the other hand, his brother Charles seems to be at home when he is abroad, for last year he made a very good innings, and on Saturday he was the only one of the eleven who secured double figures. The whole team appeared to be stiff and out of form, and the play was too bad to be correct. As usual, our old friends, Johnny MacLongstop and the Highland Chieftain, brought up at the rear, and managed to make a pair of spectacles between them. The Chieftain, who is the most persevering of cricketers, marched straight to the wicket, received one ball, and "bang went," not "saxpence," but his middle stump. The total Broughton score amounted to 37.

After a short interval given to refreshments, explanations about how the batsmen were got out, and gnashing of Wardle's teeth because Mr C Makinson would keep hitting his straight balls to the leg, the Cheetham Hill men went to the wickets, and at first it looked as if they were going to outrival their opponents in not scoring. Mr J B "Brown" (why do cricketers use pseudonyms on Saturdays?) and Mr Makinson bowled for Broughton, and Mr R Mellor was wicket-keeper too, and a very excellent wicket keeper too. Seven Cheetham Hillers went down for twenty-eight runs. Great expectations were entertained about Mr M Barlow's batting. Great expectations are often delusive, and he was given out after scoring ten, by that most ignominious of all modes of exit – leg before wicket. Mr "Brown's" bowling was very destructive, and with the aid of the wicket-keeper, Mr R Mellor, he took five wickets.

Mr J Makinson also bowled very well, but just when the interest of the match was at its height and Broughton, by a supreme effort, had a chance of winning, he appeared to tire and went off, and John Brown followed suit. Mr H Mallalieu, a young player, succeeded Mr Makinson. He bowls very straight, and promises to make a very good all-round cricketer, unless he turns it up for some less robust game like his elder brothers. Cricket, like other specialities, runs in families – to wit the Graces, the Walkers, the Rowleys, and others. Mr John Grimshaw played a good steady innings for Cheetham Hill, and carried out his bat for thirty-four. His style is somewhat pottering; but he can keep his wicket up – and that is something. As a wicket-keeper he exactly resembles Surrey Stephenson, and is very trustworthy. Wardle – the Cheetham professional – and Mr Grimshaw

won the match, the score amounting to ninety-six. Mr Mollinson is one of the few Scotchmen, in Manchester or elsewhere, who can play cricket. The game is an exotic north of the Tweed; and a friend, who had not been in Scotland, explained the matter to us by saying that there were no flat places in that country on which a wicket could be pitched.

BOWLING
BROUGHTON v CHEETHAM HILL

The fourth annual match between the bowlers of the Broughton and Cheetham Hill Cricket and Bowling Clubs was played on Thursday, last week, and on Wednesday last. The first match was played on the Broughton Green, and the return match at Cheetham Hill. For the three previous years Broughton has always been victorious; but nothing daunted, and flushed with their victories at cricket, the Cheetham Hill bowlers determined to have another tussle with their old opponents, and a home-and-home match was arranged accordingly. Last year the clubs played twelve men each, making six double and twelve single-handed games. Broughton then won by fifty-two points on their own ground, all of which in the return match Cheetham Hill wiped off, except fourteen. This was coming very close. This year the clubs increased the number of their players to sixteen on each side, but notwithstanding this the Broughton bowlers, on their own ground, only defeated their opponents by twenty-one points, which was a great falling off from the previous year, and gave the Cheetham Hillers renewed confidence that victory was at last within their grasp, and that, when they got their antagonists on their own ground at Crumpsall, they would speedily wipe off the twenty-one points, and leave a handsome surplus besides.

The return match was to have been played on Wednesday last, and the Broughton sixteen were on the ground at Crumpsall at the appointed hour, with the 'light of battle on their faces,' and eager for the fray. Their opponents did not muster in nearly such force. Unfortunately rain fell heavily during the afternoon, and after waiting patiently for several hours, the game was abandoned."

Too Many Pubs?

It would generally be thought that the number of public houses in any district is governed by the demand for drinks and the discretion of the licensing magistrates. Although we are now conditioned to accepting town planning and zoning as factors in establishing new premises of all kinds, this type of legislation is of fairly recent origin and in the last century there appeared to be little control of private enterprise in the drink trade. In Broughton, however, things were different – there was Big Brother. All the land belonged to the Clowes family and whenever it was developed they reserved rights to restrict the type of activity, apart from domestic occupancy, that might be carried on there. Such powers enabled them to plan the whole of the Broughton Estate according to their own grand design and their own ideas of what was good for the entire district and its residents.

One of their apparent dislikes was the public house, particularly where the licence provided for the sale of spirits as well as beer. They were tolerant of the "off-licence", they permitted in certain areas the "beer house", but kept a very tight grip on the opening of fully-licensed public houses. Their restriction on the type of trades and industry that might be carried on was consistent with their design to keep Broughton, particularly north of Broughton Lane, good class.

In 1887 Captain Samuel Clowes, whose "reign" from 1862 to 1899 saw Broughton's population grow from 10,000 to nearly 50,000, took action to prevent James McFarlane from converting two houses in Trafalgar Street from an "off licence" to a public house. During the course of the action, which was fought first in the Chancery Court of Lancashire, then the Court of Appeal and finally in the House of Lords, some interesting facts emerged...

1 From 1847 onwards all conveyances of land made by William Clowes, and later S W Clowes, contained this type of covenant:

"...the appointee his heirs and assigns will not erect...upon the said plot, or in any building, for the time being thereupon, any inn, tavern, or public house, or any fire engine or steam engine, vitriol work, glass work, copper work, iron foundry, dyehouse, bowking house, stove printing work, cotton or other mill or factory, lunatic asylum, or slaughter house or the trade or business of a publican, victualler, or retailer of malt, spirituous, or fermented liquors, melter of fat, pipemaker or burner, tallow chandler, soap boiler, chairmaker, currier, brewer, distiller, sugar baker, working brazier, tinman, dyer, stover, dresser, or any structure, work, trade, business, or employment, whether the kind hereinbefore specified or not, which is, can, or may be deemed a public nuisance or private inconvenience to the neighbourhood, or which may lessen the value of the lands lying near the said plot or of any building thereon; and further, will not build a meeting house or chapel."

2 In the whole of Broughton only three fully licensed houses were opened in 40 years after 1847. They were the Royal Archer and the Vavasour in Lower Broughton and the purpose-built Broughton Hotel on Great Cheetham Street East, a good distance away from the others. There were five older houses on which there were no restricting covenants, making only eight in all. Both Colonel Clowes and his son, Captain Clowes, had constantly objected to any fully-licensed premises on the estate. In addition, there were only 18 beer houses, none of which could sell spirits, and only four of these were north of Broughton Lane.

In the Chancery Court, the Vice Chancellor refused to grant an injunction to Captain Clowes, accepting the arguments of Mr McFarlane's counsel that because all the covenants throughout Broughton had not been enforced, then this one should not be invoked. Works of different kinds had been set up without complaint and so had many off licences. When Captain Clowes gave notice of Appeal, many people who thought they might be affected if he won were very worried and called a meeting at the Royal Archer to rally support. Those attending included local property owners and many licencees and their trade associations. They feared the re-affirmation of what they thought were old and abandoned covenants against businesses which they had built up both in the drink and other trades. A memorandum was drawn up, asking Captain Clowes to withdraw his Appeal. But this was in vain and the Court of Appeal overturned the Chancery Court decision and granted the injunction. Mr McFarlane took the case to the

Lords but was unsuccessful. The judgement was to the effect that waiving rights in one part of the estate did not affect the power to enforce them in other parts. Although a breach of covenant could be overlooked in one place, a similar breach could be successfully resisted elsewhere. The Clowes' traditional belief that pubs lowered the standards of the neighbourhood coloured their approach to every application for a new one, and their opposition was stronger the nearer each new proposal was to Higher Broughton's select acres. In the more crowded areas they were more understanding of the function of beer houses. Similar considerations applied to commercial premises; factories providing employment for the working people were welcome enough in Lower Broughton, but few such enterprises ever flourished further north.

That these powers of control were vested in one man was most unusual, but he was the sole landowner and so his position differed from that of landowners in neighbouring Salford, Pendleton, Cheetham, Crumpsall or Prestwich. In most places the land was in several different hands, and even where large holdings were involved the owners were not all of one mind regarding development. In Broughton the Clowes' planning powers were a century ahead of their time and were probably as great as those possessed by local or central government of this day.

Cheetham Hill 100 years ago

THE SPHINX.

Most Manchester residents will scarcely require informing that if they get on the 'bus which starts from the Bull's Head Passage, in Corporation Street, it will take them, if they choose, to Cheetham Hill; but few specimens of the 'civis Mancuniensis' know how interesting a history attaches to that village. Cheetham Hill has a long and honourable story of its own, and our only present regret is that want of space will not permit that story to be told here. It is only possible to indicate, as it were, the heads of the subject.

The district known conventionally as Cheetham Hill lies north-east of a line drawn through Elizabeth Street, and includes Hightown, Tetlow Fold, Crumpsall, part of Broughton Park, and the Village proper. A century ago the village was quite unattached from Manchester, and was a pleasant incident on the way from the latter place to Bury. It had little connection with Manchester, except that the handloom weavers who worked in it went to the town for their warps and weft. Forty years ago it had distinctly assumed the character of a suburb of Manchester; the weavers were few, and as now, most of the inhabitants had business in the town, and resorted to the village as a healthy and handy country residence. At that time the place was a garden, with odd houses, and odd rows of houses, dotted here and there. Barring the main road to Bury, the place seems never to have been planned, and to this day is as labyrinthian as Knicker-Bockers' New Amsterdam, planned by the cows. Its streets wind about in the most inconsequential manner. It has short-cut passages with most unpromising beginnings, and many likely-looking roads which turn out to be impasses, if we may borrow a much-needed word from the French. Its inhabitants should be pretty good in point of morals and religion. To begin with, there is St Luke's, built early in the century when the taste in Church architecture was beginning to revive; then there is St Mary's, built when the aforesaid taste had somewhat revived, an edifice nearly beautiful, its salient lines Early English, with ornament and tracery of a later period; next St Mark's, about the most unpretentiously ugly building in the United Kingdom, a horrid brick structure, which would be complimented by being called a barn, and which was built in the heathen period of the Church of England, when the chief gods worshipped in the land were ugliness, cheapness, cockfighting, bull-baiting, brandied wines, and - the devil in various other shapes; then, a shade better, there is the Wesleyan Chapel, built about eighty years ago, brick and ugly; and lastly, there is rising up in Hightown, a new Church of St John, which with its parsonage will be an ornament.

Besides these places of worship there are several schools, so that education and morality are pretty well provided for. It is simply a duty to say that the manners and customs of the place are accordingly orderly and respectable, the inhabitants highly so.

Let us have a line or two of history. If you turn up Crescent Road, at the corner of the 'bus office, go along on the right hand side until you nearly reach a lane called Humphrey Street, you will find a brick wall round a good-sized garden. That wall encloses a site on which stood, about forty years ago, a timber-framed house, which was the birthplace, and for sometime the residence, of glorious old Humphrey Chetham, whose goodness of heart and soundness of head founded the College and Library at Hunt's Bank.

Cheetham Hill seems to have been for centuries celebrated for archery, and there is still a bow and arrow maker's shop here. At least one other old arrow maker lives still in the village, but he does not now follow that craft.

To sustain the inner man Cheetham Hill has ample provision in numerous shops containing eatables or drinkables. Among the inns, appropriately first, comes the old Staff of Life, now called the Crumpsall Arms. It is presided over by a lady who a dozen years ago ruled in "the Ditch" and was the cynosure of business men from the Corn and Royal Exchanges, the ceaseless motley throng which on Tuesday and Friday afternoons invades the Spread Eagle.

The Crumpsall Hotel contains a comfortable, old-fashioned smoking room, which is frequented chiefly by old-stagers, quiet, responsible-looking, respectable men, who come regularly, always sit down in the same corner, smoke churchwarden clays, and drink comforting drinks in a solemn and important style. They talk freely and agreeably, settle all things they want putting straight, and compare notes about their gardens and new-laid eggs. Perhaps the favourite topic is gardens and garden produce. Opposite the 'bus office is a public-house which is so modest as not to have up its name. Whatever it may be called now, it used to be the Robin Hood. A more miscellaneous company resorts hither, many wayfarers call in, and expectant 'bus passengers take their nips. Nearer town, on the opposite side, is the Bird-in-Hand, an old house, a favourite place of call for carters for a century nearly. The stocks used to be near this house. In front of it is a watering-trough and rarely does the passer-by fail to see carters' carts waiting at the door.

The aristocratic house of the village is the Griffin, which has been a good old-fashioned hotel for more than a century. The Griffin Bowling Green has existed more than that length of time. A dozen years ago the house showed two roofs to the front; the gables are now built up. How many archery and bowling dinners have been held in this house during this and the last centuries, nobody can tell; but the house has long been celebrated for those things, nay still is for bowlers, and for the occasional Friday evening tripe-suppers formerly a regular institution here. The house, fifty years ago, was a great place of resort of the 'quality' of Cheetham Hill. Here great dinner parties and balls were held, and here came the aristocratic old bucks to spend their evenings socially together. The company usually frequenting the house in these days consists of tradesmen, merchants, and that grade of people which, for want of a better word, can only be described as 'highly respectable'. Lastly, there is the 'Temple', near St Luke's, quiet looking outside, a snug place inside, patronized by Smedley and Hightown. A racy sort of character about the company meeting here lends sometimes a charm to an hour.

But there are higher things to talk about in Cheetham Hill. Do not the Mayor and the Bishop reside there? And is not Cheetham Hill proud, and justly so, on that account? Are there not artists, journalists, merchant princes, bankers, and goodness knows who besides? The late Mr Loyd lived at Greenhill, a fine house now pulled down, its site undergoing excavation for a new road. By the way, it should be mentioned that the church of St John, in Waterloo Road, already described, is being erected as a memorial to the deceased banker, by his son.

Perhaps no immediate suburb of Manchester has close around it so many beautiful walks as Cheetham Hill. Broughton Park and Heaton Park are close to; and what a splendid road is the Bury Old Road! Half an hour's walk will take one to Kersal Moor or to Queen's Park; in fact, for a pleasant outing you can't go in the wrong direction - unless you turn towards town. The cricketing and bowling greens of the Cheetham Hill Club are pleasantly situated behind St Mary's Church, and are only spoiled by the ugly back of some ugly brick houses which confront one side of the cricket field. The cricket season here is to be opened by a match this week between Cheetham Hill and Broughton. May the day be fine, and 'may we be there to see!'"

Two walks into history
1 Cheetham Hill

Demolition and rebuilding have obliterated most of the places and buildings described in this book, but fortunately in 1984 we still have many fine specimens of the olden days and a very interesting afternoon's walk could commence at the town end of Cheetham Hill Road. Here you will find St Chad's Roman Catholic Church, dating from 1847, and the Cheetham Town Hall, completed in 1852 and recently renovated but no longer in municipal use. The Knowsley Hotel (now renamed the Derby Brewery Arms) is from the same period and the offices of the Prestwich Union bear the date 1862. This building is a reminder of the days of the Poor Law, when several local districts in North Manchester, including Cheetham, amalgamated as the Prestwich Union "to relieve the poor" and this was their headquarters. Immediately opposite, in a derelict state awaiting a buyer for any purpose, is the former Great Synagogue, which was consecrated in 1858 and in use for a century until there were no longer any Jews living near enough for regular services.

There are still many old properties along Cheetham Hill Road now in use as warehouses and offices which are over a hundred years old. A stone bearing the inscription "Temple Terrace" is still clearly visible just past Broughton Street; the remaining houses are now used as showrooms by a firm selling bathroom furniture but they were once fine residences, among the first to be built here about 1840.

Continuing up the road, note the Temple Hotel (c1855) and whatever remains of the most "fashionable" church of Victorian and Edwardian Cheetham, St Luke's, which was consecrated in 1839 and on whose magnificent organ Mendelssohn played a few years later. Nearby, at the corner of Smedley Lane, note an old mansion close to the road, Birds Cliff, built about the same time as the church and owned by one of the leaders of the Manchester Council, Alderman Bake, who lived there for most of the mid-nineteenth century. The big houses of this period along Cheetham Hill Village have all gone, but St Mark's Church (1790) saw them built and has survived them. Standing near to the boundaries of Cheetham, Broughton and Crumpsall, the church is no longer in use, nor is the nearby building which bears the plaque "St Mark's School, 1815". The Robin Hood Hotel, its neighbour and contemporary, is still open. In 1794 this was known as the Shooting Butt Green and Bowling Green and was owned and occupied by Benjamin Slinger. (The present owners, Wilsons Brewery, very kindly extracted this information from the title deeds.) All the remaining property in and around St Mark's Lane, although long ago converted into shops and offices, dates from the early 1800's. They include Union Terrace, the busy row of shops, and Bank House at the corner of George Street, now a china and glass warehouse and shop. After the Half Way House, between Melton Road and Park Road, houses were built about 1850 for the merchants and businessmen; Holly House, Heaton Terrace and Heaton Villas are still occupied, mostly as flats. The tour ends with three stately homes, High Bank at the corner of

Scholes Lane, now known as Nazareth House, dating from the end of the eighteenth century; Heaton Hall in Heaton Park, a perfect example of a country house of the 1770's, and in Scholes Lane there is the former Prestwich Town Hall. This was built as a residence about 1850 in the classical style favoured a century earlier and now stands empty awaiting tenants for the offices into which it has been converted. The estate agents describe it as Prestwich Old Hall, but it has never been known by this name and the original gateposts bear the name of Bent Hill.

2 Broughton

There are also a few reminders of the glory of the early and mid-Victorian age on Bury New Road, and if we start at the Grove Inn we have a reminder of the horse-drawn lorries for which the road was built. This inn, dating back over a hundred and fifty years, has recently been renovated and enlarged, but it was, until the 1930's, a favourite last "pull-up" for the horses before their journey's end in town. A little higher up the hill, at the corner of Great Cheetham Street, just one house of a lovely terrace has been preserved and at the corner of Great Clowes Street a hundred yards or so away there is another very good example of an 1840 house which is still occupied. St John's Church off Wellington Street was the first church to be built in Broughton and its principal benefactor, John Clowes, was buried there. Only one terrace of the houses in which some of its worshippers would have lived remains and this is Belmont, now converted into many offices. Opposite is the Greek Church, built by the merchants who made Higher Broughton their home. Now note another reminder of horse-drawn traffic at the corner of Knoll Street. Here for many years were the stables belonging to the omnibus

Cheetham Hill Village

companies and there were tramlines curving from the main road. The company name is still clearly visible carved on the front of the building.

Knoll Street leads via Hope Street to Lower Broughton Road, and a short distance to the left look out for the name Scarr Wheel carved on the wall and gate posts. This led to the seventeenth century home of the astronomer William Crabtree. At the end of the path a blue plaque was recently erected to commemorate him. A new house was built there a few years ago which has a magnificent view of the bend of the River Irwell and is a reminder that the river bank was the site of cottages and smallholdings in the distant past. Some very fine houses on Lower Broughton Road were reputedly built in Regency times and Cliff House, the last before the junction with Great Clowes Street, is a good example.

We are now at the point where the road caved in over fifty years ago, permanently blocking the roadway leading into Bury New Road, and known locally as "the landslide".

There is, however, a footpath and we can continue up the hill towards Kersal. In Radford Street there were some fine mansions and Kersal Bank still provides us with well preserved houses which are typical of the 1840's. On the main road at the corner of Moor Lane is the first and only shop after Newbury Place. Originally the toll house, it has been a newsagent/tobacconist's for a hundred years since the toll was abolished. The famous St Paul's Church and Churchyard is in Moor Lane around the corner and has a history of over a hundred and thirty years. This pales into insignificance when we go down Moor Lane to Littleton Road and see Kersal Cell, whose history goes back many hundreds of years. After four hundred years of religious use, it was a private house for three hundred years and is now a restaurant. Here we have gone much further back in time than anywhere else on our tours and it is a fitting conclusion to the walks into history.

Why Leicester Road was built

Leicester Road, Salford, was born because the Prestwich Council wanted a tramways system. The junction of Leicester Road with Bury Old Road and its continuation as Middleton Road is one of the busiest crossroads in North Manchester. The volume of traffic in Leicester Road is dense throughout the day and at peak times cars, vans, heavy lorries and buses form long tail-backs from the intersection. All forms of vehicle pass along the road, except the trams, for which it was originally created, and they disappeared without trace many years ago. Records show that in 1902 the development of Leicester Road was planned to fulfil and agreement to provide Prestwich and Middleton with tramway connections to Salford and Manchester.

In those earliest days of the electric tramcar, the Councils of Manchester and Salford had taken over the routes along their own roads operated by the privately owned Manchester Carriage and Tramway Company and had agreed inter-running rights. Salford, however, had obtained the contract to build the Prestwich tramways and run them for 21 years along both Bury New Road and Bury Old Road. The former route was an easy task, as it meant only an extension from Kersal, but to run along Bury Old Road required a direct link between Great Cheetham Street West and Half Way House public house. A somewhat tortuous route lay along Great Cheetham Street East, Tetlow Lane and George Street and in fact the Council had studied the feasibility of widening these roads to enable tramcars to join the Manchester system along part

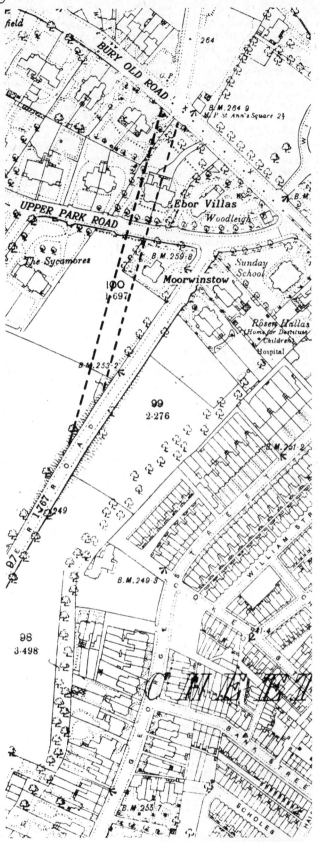

of Bury Old Road. This scheme proved too costly and the Tramway Committee devised the Leicester Road Extension, which received Council approval in November 1902. This meant building a new road, complete with tramlines, connecting Great Cheetham Street with Bury Old Road but making use of such roads as were already there. Wilfred Street was part of a large area of streets of identical terraced cottages and it led from Great Cheetham Street East to Devonshire Street, crossing Warwick Street and Worcester Street. One side of this street was demolished to widen it and became the first section. A little further north a few houses had recently been built and named Leicester Street, which included Leicester Terrace (still in good condition today and showing a plaque dated 1899). After this there were only fields until Broom Lane where Leicester Road began and this curved to join Upper Park Road near its beginning. There was no break in either Bury Old Road or Upper Park Road and as yet, of course, no crossroads.

The new section of road was built from Devonshire Street to Broom Lane, joining together Wilfred Street, Leicester Street and what was then Leicester Road. But in order to meet Middleton Road a further section was needed. This was the most complicated operation of all, since it meant demolition of property in Upper Park Road and the swallowing up of some of the grounds of other houses. The evidence of this act of urban surgery is still visible. One of a pair of grand semi-detached residences known as Ebor Villas was the victim, but its other half was spared and still shows the scar of its separation on Leicester Road, where the gable end abuts the pavement. The name was changed to Kinderton and after being a residence for many years it is now a synagogue. The large house, Moorwinstow, stands in an unusual triangular plot of land between Leicester Road and Leicester Avenue and this was also a consequence of the extension, since most of its original grounds now form part of the carriage-way.

The whole of the work, from Council approval to operation of the tramway system, took only two years and by the end of 1904 a direct line from Salford to Prestwich via Leicester Road was in regular use. Wilfred Street and Leicester Street were renamed Leicester Road and the old part to Upper Park Road became Leicester Avenue.

St Chad's, Cheetham, in 1850

APPENDIX 1

1824 inhabitants

A directory of 1824 includes the following names:

Appleton Misses Eliza and Ann, Temple Cottage, Cheetham Hill (1)

Ashley Mary, Miller, Kersall Moor (2)

Ashton George, Calenderer. house, Smedley

Atherton Mrs Ann, Gentlewoman, Kersall Cell (3)

Barker Jos, Tailor, White Smithy-bar, Crumpsall (4)

Barlow John, Shopkeeper, Sandy Lane (5)

Bates Charles, Constable and Overseer, Nett lane, Cheetham Hill

Blair and Yates, Calico Printers, Irwell Bank, Agecroft

Boardman John, Gentleman, Smedley Lane

Burns Samuel, Victualler, Eagle and Child bowling green, Temple, Cheetham Hill (1)

Byron Miss E, Gentlewoman, Kersal Cell (3)

Chippendale John, Calico Printer, Beech Hill, Smedley

Christie Robert, Drysalter, Broomfield, Cheetham Hill (6)

Clowes Rev John, Broughton Hall, Broughton (7)

Deans A R & S, Victualler, Robin Hood and bowling green

Edge Samuel, Attorney, Broomfield, Cheetham Hill (6)

Ethelston Rev C W, Magistrate, Smedley Hill

Fletcher George, Victualler, Griffin Inn and bowling green, Cheetham Hill

Garnett Robert, Merchant, Oak Hill, Cheetham Hill

Garnett William, Merchant, Tetlow Fold (8)

Grimshaw Jas, Fustian Manufacturer, Broughton Bridge

Grundy George, Manufacturer, Tetlow Fold, Cheetham Hill (8)

Hammond James, Chain Maker & Smith, White Smithy Bar (4)

Henshaw Mrs S, Gentlewoman, Stonewall, Cheetham Hill (9)

Hibbert Jas Esq, Magistrate, Broughton House, Broughton (10)

Howarth Edmond, Calico Printer, Smedley Bank, Cheetham

Jackson John, Victualler, Bird in Hand, Cheetham Hill

Johnson Thos, Manufacturer, Smedley Lane, Cheetham Hill

Kirkman John, Temple, Cheetham Hill (1)

Lee John, Commercial School, Chapel Lane, Cheetham Hill

Leicester Mrs Ellen, Gentlewoman, Kersall Hall

Leicester Jas, Victualler, Griffin and Turf Tavern, Kersall Moor (11)

Lewis David, Turkey Red Dyer, Smedley

Lowe Miss Sarah, Ladies Boarding School, Broughton

Loyd Edward Esq, Banker, Greenhill, Cheetham Hill

Mather G B, Nankeen Manufacturer, Smedley Lane, Cheetham Hill

Pilkington Edmond, Bow and Arrow Maker, Cheetham Hill

Potter Benjamin, Merchant, Tetlow Fold, Cheetham Hill (8)

Potter Richard Esq, Brewer, Smedley Hall, Cheetham Hill

Scholes James Esq, Tetlow Fold, Cheetham Hill (8)

Sergeant Mrs Elizabeth, Sandy Bank, Crumpsall (12)

Shore Wm, Cotton Merchant, Sandybank, Crumpsall (12)

Smith Nathaniel, Draper, Smedley Lane, Cheetham

Taylor Mrs Mary, Rycroft House, Crumpsall (13)

Taylor Thos, Fustian Manufacturer, Smedley Lane

Thackaray Daniel, Gentleman, Sandy Bank, Crumpsall (12)

Thorley Cadman, Scotch Warehouse, Smedley

Thornton George, Toll Bar Keeper, Smedley Lane End

Tyson Mrs Grace, St Mark Street, Cheetham Hill